W9-AGI-350

ENCYCLOPEDIA OF MAMMALS

VOLUME 11
Ora–Pol

MARSHALL CAVENDISH
NEW YORK • LONDON • TORONTO • SYDNEY

ORANGUTANS

ZEFA

OLD MAN OF THE FOREST

THE LAST OF THE GREAT APES TO BE FOUND OUTSIDE AFRICA, THE TREE-DWELLING, SOLITARY ORANGUTAN IS A FASCINATING BUT, UNFORTUNATELY, ENDANGERED CREATURE

A glimpse of shaggy red fur through the trees, the groan of a tree branch bending under a great weight, the deep, unmistakable sound of a burbling burp. All these signs may betray the presence of one of the world's most extraordinary animals—the mighty orangutan of the rain forests of Sumatra and Borneo.

In the Malayan language, the name orangutan means "old man of the forest" and there is a host of stories and folktales surrounding this magnificent creature. One legend says that orangutans are really people who dare not speak for fear of being put to work. Other stories also stress the orangutan's humanlike features and qualities. One tale tells of how humans were created by birdlike creatures. The creatures fell asleep and, when they woke up, found that they could not remember exactly how to make humans anymore. The closest they could get was to produce a shaggy-haired creature that

Orangutans are primates. This order is divided into two major groups—the lower primates, or prosimians, and the higher primates, or simians. The higher primates include the monkeys and apes. The apes are further split into two families—the Hylobatidae, or lesser apes (gibbons), and the Pongidae, or great apes (gorillas, chimpanzees, and orangutans).

ORDER
Primates

FOUR SPECIES IN THREE GENERA

FAMILY
Pongidae

GENUS
Pongo pygmaeus

SUBSPECIES
Pongo pygmaeus pygmaeus
(Bornean orangutan)
Pongo pygmaeus abelii
(Sumatran orangutan)

somewhat resembled a human being. Many 16th-century European explorers, the first to see orangutans in the wild, were also struck by their similarity to human beings. An 18th-century scientist, Lord Monbodo, even wrote that the orangutan's character and disposition were "sufficient to denominate him a man." Their suspicions were to prove correct. We know now that orangutans and the other great apes—the gorillas and chimpanzees—are our closest relatives on the evolutionary tree, although orangutans are less "human" than their cousins.

The first known primates appeared on earth some 70 million years ago. They were probably

---

IN 1971, AN ART COMPETITION IN KANSAS WAS WON BY DJAKARTA JIM, A SIX-YEAR-OLD ORANGUTAN FROM TOPEKA ZOO

---

insect-eaters and looked similar to the tree shrews of today. Over the next 30 to 40 million years, they were displaced in many regions by monkeys and eventually by the earliest known apes. The apes differed from the early primates in the way they swung through the trees rather than scampered across the branches. Physical changes reflected this change in lifestyle—the apes evolved longer arms for swinging and lost their tails, as these were no longer essential for balance or grip. Instead,

Orangutans are unsociable, solitary apes, unlike chimpanzees and gorillas, which live in close-knit family groups.

The two subspecies of orangutan, from Borneo and Sumatra, share the characteristic shaggy red coats (left).

Carl Purcell/Colorific

The orangutan spends little time on the ground, having evolved as a tree dweller, with long arms and big, powerful hands (above).

they developed hugely powerful hands and feet for holding on to the branches. They also developed larger and more complex brains than their ancestors and came to rely much more on their eyesight for judging distances than their sense of smell for finding their way around. From these great apes, another primate eventually evolved— *Homo sapiens*, or human beings.

HABITS AND HABITAT

Orangutans are found only on the islands of Borneo and Sumatra in Southeast Asia. They were once much more widespread but are now restricted to small pockets of forests. The two groups have developed into separate subspecies— *Pongo pygmaeus pygmaeus* in Borneo and *Pongo pygmaeus abelii* in Sumatra. The Sumatran orangutan has a longer, lighter coat and males have bushy beards and mustaches.

Orangutans are the most arboreal of the great apes, spending most of their time up in the trees, searching for fruit to eat or simply resting. They are among the heaviest of all tree-living animals. Adult males can weigh as much as 165 lb (75 kg); adult females are about half their size. Even the sturdiest branches sometimes crack under their weight, as the many signs of broken bones in a survey of orangutan skeletons testified. Despite their great size, orangutans are superbly adapted to their life in the trees. Physically, they have long, strong, curved

Joseph Van Wormer/Bruce Coleman Ltd.

fingers and toes for keeping a firm grip of the branches. They have very long arms to enable swinging along under the branches, although these make them seem relatively clumsy movers on the ground. Orangutans spend their nights up in the trees, too, weaving themselves cozy sleeping nests from springy branches and twigs.

An orangutan's day consists mainly of searching for and eating food. Orangutans are fruit eaters, plucking off fruit and pulling it open with their strong fingers and thumbs. When fruit is scarce, they will also eat nuts, bark, seeds, and the

ORANGUTAN MOTHERS ARE KILLED BY POACHERS WHO STEAL THE BABIES, WHICH FETCH HIGH PRICES AS EXOTIC PETS

occasional bird's egg. When they are thirsty, they lick the rainwater from leaves or scoop rainwater up from hollow tree trunks with their hands.

Orangutans were once widespread throughout Asia. Today, however, there may be fewer than 30,000 left in the wild. As the human population increases, the orangutans' forest home is being destroyed to make way for houses and farms, and for valuable timber products. However, the governments of both Indonesia and Malaysia have now established reserves where orangutans are protected and where orphaned orangutans are rehabiliated. Orangutans have also been successfully bred in captivity and there is a worldwide attempt in progress to insure the conservation of these fascinating animals. ∎

ⒶNCESTORS

The orangutan is the only great ape found in Asia. Today, it is restricted to small patches of rain forest in Sumatra and Borneo. In prehistoric times, however, it was found on the Asian mainland too, ranging from Java to southern China. The earliest known ape fossils come from Egypt and date back about 27 million years. But it is thought that the orangutan evolved from an early Asian ape, either *Ramapithecus* or *Sivapithecus*, whose fossils were first found in India. They evolved about 15 million years ago.

THE ORANGUTAN'S FAMILY TREE

The primate order is generally split into two major groups—the prosimians, or lesser primates (such as lemurs, lorises, and galagos), and the simians, or higher primates (which include monkeys, apes, and human beings). There are 14 species of ape, divided into the lesser apes, or Hylobatidae (gibbons), and the great apes, or Pongidae (the orangutans, chimpanzees, and gorillas).

OLD WORLD MONKEYS

NEW WORLD MONKEYS

HUMANS

Peter David Scott/Wildlife Art Agency

COMMON CHIMPANZEE

GORILLA

ORANGUTAN
Pongo pygmaeus
(*PONG-o PIG-mayuss*)

The orangutan belongs to the Pongidae family of great apes. Together with the chimpanzees and gorillas, they are our closest relatives. The two subspecies of orangutan live in the tropical rain forests of lowland Borneo and northern Sumatra, where, through trapping and habitat destruction, only about 30,000 remain and they are now classed as endangered. Orangutans are the most arboreal of the great apes, superbly adapted to a life up in the trees, where they search for fruit and build their sleeping nests.

GREAT APES

APES

APE FORMS

GIBBONS

PROSIMIANS

MONKEYS

PRIMATES

1541

ANATOMY: THE ORANGUTAN

There is a vast difference in size between the sexes, with males weighing in at about 165 lb (75 kg) and females at about 88 lb (40 kg). Adult males stand 5 ft (1.5 m) tall; females 3 ft (1 m) tall. A tall human male stands about 6 ft (2 m) tall.

EYES, BRAIN, AND FACE

Forward-facing eyes allow orangutans to judge distances well, and relatively large brains allow excellent coordination, vital requirements for a tree-dwelling creature. Males (above left) grow beards or mustaches, and face flaps develop between the ages of twelve and fourteen. The female face (above right) is relatively hairless.

HANDS

Orangutans show greater mechanical aptitude and manual dexterity than chimpanzees do (in captivity), being able to undo nuts and bolts that would fool a chimpanzee.

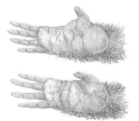

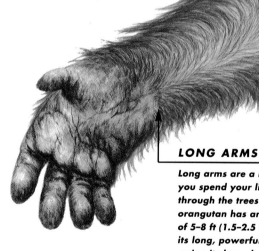

EARS

Orangutans have the flat ears that are typical of primates. Hearing is all-important as adult males (male ear— near left) keep each other informed of their whereabouts through screeches and barking.

LONG ARMS

Long arms are a necessity if you spend your life swinging through the trees. An orangutan has an arm span of 5–8 ft (1.5–2.5 m). It uses its long, powerful arms to swing its large body through the trees, underneath the branches, and to reach fruit.

Illustrations Guy Troughton

The orangutan has a skeleton adapted for vertical posture. Features include a short back, broad rib cage, and sturdy pelvis. The orangutan's arms are considerably longer than its legs to make it easier to swing through the forest trees. You can tell apes from monkeys by their lack of a tail.

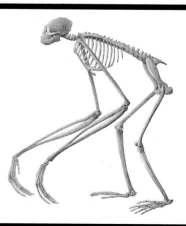

Orangutans have broad, powerful feet and hands for gripping and grasping. They have long, strong, hook-shaped fingers and toes, with shorter, opposable thumbs and big toes for greater mobility. The nails are flat and blunt.

HAND   FOOT

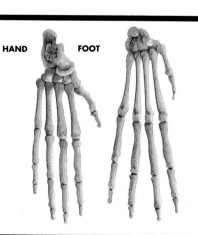

X-ray illustrations Elisabeth Smith

T H E   O R A N G - U T A N

CLASSIFICATION

FAMILY: PONGIDAE

GENUS AND SPECIES: *PONGO PYGMAEUS*

SUBSPECIES: *PONGO PYGMAEUS*
PYGMAEUS (BORNEO)

PONGO PYGMAEUS ABELII (SUMATRA)

SIZE

HEIGHT/MALE: 5 FT (1.5 M)

HEIGHT/FEMALE: 3 FT (1 M)

WEIGHT/MALE: 165 LB (75 KG)

WEIGHT/FEMALE: 88 LB (40 KG)

WEIGHT AT BIRTH: 3 LB (1.5 KG)

ON AVERAGE, MALES ARE TWICE THE SIZE OF FEMALES

COLORATION

REDDISH BROWN COATS BUT RANGES FROM BRIGHT
ORANGE IN YOUNG TO DARK BROWN IN SOME
ADULTS; LIGHTER IN SUMATRAN ORANGS; DARKER IN
ZOO-BRED ORANGS. ADULTS HAVE BLACK
FACES; YOUNG HAVE PINK MUZZLES AND PINK SKIN
AROUND THEIR EYES

FEATURES

AS THEY GET OLDER, MALES DEVELOP LARGE, FATTY
CHEEK PADS (WHICH ENHANCE THEIR AGGRESSIVE
DISPLAYS) AND INFLATABLE THROAT POUCHES

   VERY LONG ARM SPAN—5–8 FT (1.5–2.5 M)
FROM FINGERTIP TO FINGERTIP (FOR ARBOREAL
LOCOMOTION)

   LARGE BRAINS FOR THEIR SIZE; HIGHLY
INTELLIGENT

   THE HEAVIEST TREE-LIVING ANIMAL

   LIFE SPAN: 30–40 YEARS

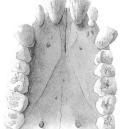

SKIN
In younger orangutans, the skin on
the muzzle and around the eyes is
pinkish. In adults, the facial skin
is bare and completely black.

COAT
Orangutans are famous for their striking
appearance, thanks mainly to their long, shaggy
coats of reddish brown hair. Sumatran
orangutans have longer, lighter hair than their
Bornean cousins, and males tend to have longer
hair than females. Sumatran males also have
conspicuous mustaches and beards.

LOWER MANDIBLE

The orangutan's large jaws and
molars are adapted for grinding
tough plants, nuts, and bark.

**MALE SKULL
(SIDE VIEW)**

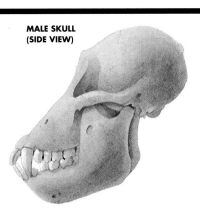

SKULLS
Orangutans' skulls
have a relatively large
brain capacity, being
up to 27 c in (450 cc) in
volume. Their brains
are about as large as
those of chimpanzees.

**FEMALE SKULL
(SIDE VIEW)**

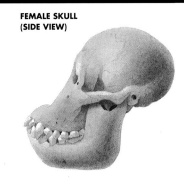

LONERS OF THE FOREST

MORE AND MORE IS BEING FOUND ABOUT THE ENDANGERED ORANGUTAN, DESPITE THE FACT THAT IT IS THE MOST INTROVERTED AND ANTISOCIAL OF THE GREAT APES

Deep in the hot, steamy jungle, a large, red, shaggy-haired ape sits high up in a tree, leisurely pulling out the fleshy pulp of a durian fruit with its large lips and long fingers. An orangutan having a snack of one of its favorite foods. Having had its fill of that particular tree's fruit supply, it slowly and deliberately swings its great bulk through the trees in search of its next meal. This is the pattern of much of an orangutan's typical day—a snack, followed by a short journey or a rest, then another snack, followed by another short journey or another rest.

An orangutan begins its day at dawn, when it leaves its temporary sleeping nest high up in a tree. It builds a new nest each night, to provide a clean, comfortable bed of springy branches, twigs, and

---

SOME OLD MALE ORANGUTANS BECOME TOO HEAVY TO LIVE IN THE TREES AND SPEND MOST OF THE TIME ON THE GROUND

---

leaves. It has a quick breakfast of whatever fruit its sleeping tree has to offer, then a short rest to prepare itself for the day ahead.

When it is time to move off, the orangutan gingerly tests each branch before it trusts it with its considerable weight. If the branch is strong enough, the orangutan begins its journey through the trees, swinging from branch to branch, using its long arms and its long, strong fingers and toes to keep a firm grip. At the next fruit-bearing tree on its route, it stops for a quick snack, or a longer feed if there is plenty of fruit to be had, and the whole, slow process begins again.

It take a great deal of food to fuel a body as big as an orangutan's, which explains why the animal has to spend a large part of its day searching for

and eating food. The bulk of its diet consists of tropical fruits, such as figs, mangoes, litchis, and spiky durian fruits.

Unlike the other great apes, orangutans are solitary animals, spending most of their lives on their own. Even if a group assembles in a particularly

The orang's day is a leisurely pattern of resting, feeding and foraging, nest building, and sleeping (below).

Konrad Wothe/Oxford Scientific Films

When fruit is in short supply, orangutans supplement their diet with tree bark, leaves and shoots, insects, and the occasional bird's egg (right).

Gerald Cubitt/Bruce Coleman Ltd.

Young orangutans (above) *are more sociable than their elders and are often seen playing in groups.*

well-stocked fruit tree, the individuals will take very little notice of one another, arriving, leaving, and feeding quite separately. Only the young seem to enjoy each other's company, playing and indulging in mock fights on the rare occasions that they meet. The males are the most antisocial of all, only seeking out the company of females in order to mate. They play no part in the upbringing of their offspring or in their family life. Indeed, they do their best to avoid contact even with each other.

Despite their solitary lifestyles, orangutans are highly intelligent, resourceful animals, capable of amazing feats of memory and learning. In the wild, they can remember, with extraordinary accuracy, the exact locations and fruiting seasons of a whole range of trees.

SIGN LANGUAGE

Captive orangutans have been taught to use human sign language with great success. A male orangutan raised at the University of Tennessee always used a special sign meaning "dirty" when he wanted to go to the toilet. He also used the same sign to trick his trainers into letting him go to the bathroom so that he could play with bars of soap!

Until fairly recently, little was known about the behavior and lifestyle of orangutans, partly because of their solitary natures and partly because of their isolated habitat. They are much less sociable and far more introverted than their cousins the chimpanzees, for example, and consequently far more difficult to study. In recent years, however, extensive studies both in zoos and in the wild have been carried out and we now know far more about these spectactular creatures. This increased interest in and study of orangutans has also served to highlight their plight as an endangered species. ■

Gerry Ellis

HABITATS

O rangutans were once found all over Asia. Today, they are restricted to just two areas of Southeast Asia—the islands of Borneo and Sumatra. The subspecies *Pongo pygmaeus pygmaeus* is found in Borneo; *Pongo pygmaeus abelii* lives in Sumatra. On both islands, the orangutan's habitats are being destroyed at an alarming pace to clear space for building and agriculture.

In Borneo and Sumatra, the orangutans inhabit small patches of tropical rain forest, mountain forest, and mangrove swamps. Their main requirements of their habitat are fruit trees as their chief source of

Orangutans are arboreal (tree-dwelling) animals (right and below). They swing slowly through the trees in search of food and remain there to sleep and breed. Only adult males spend much time on the forest floor.

Konrad Wothe/Oxford Scientific Films

C. & R. Aveling/ICCE

DISTRIBUTION

Orangutans have an extremely restricted distribution, being found in only two small regions of the world—Borneo and Sumatra. On Borneo, they live in small areas of primary rain forest in the states of Sabah, Sarawak, and Kalimantan. On Sumatra, they are found in a small patch of jungle in Atjeh, a mountainous region in the northwest of the island.

KEY

▪ ORANGUTAN

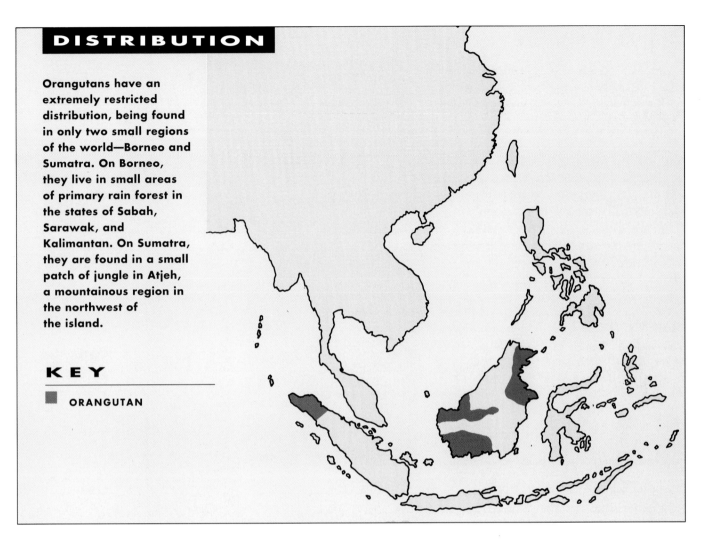

food and suitable trees for building their sleeping nests. Nests are made of branches and leaves and are usually built about 33–66 ft (10–20 m) above the ground. The nest is occupied for only a few nights before a new one is built elsewhere.

The orangutans spend most of the time in the lower to middle branches of the trees, although they do venture higher up from time to time. Their huge size means that, apart from humans,

> ORANGS USUALLY REACT TO HUMAN
> INTRUDERS BY SHOWERING THEM WITH
> BRANCHES—DIRECT ATTACKS ARE RARE

they have almost no natural enemies. Sumatran orangutans are occasionally hunted by tigers, but there are so few of these cats left that they do not pose a serious threat.

The rain forest provides a very stable environment for the orangutans. It is hot and humid all year round, with very little difference in temperature between the seasons. Rather than seasons, the

KEY FACTS

● If an orangutan cannot reach the next branch with its hands, it rocks the tree it is sitting in to and fro until the branch is within grabbing distance.

● In general, primates are concentrated in the tropical parts of the world. Large areas of the globe have no nonhuman primate representatives at all.

● Most orangutans make only rare excursions down to the forest floor. But older, heavier males sometimes find it easier to "fist-walk" along the ground than to find branches strong enough to bear their great weight.

● There is evidence to suggest that adult males continue their aggressive behavior even after they have ceased to be sexually active after about thirty years. The reason for this is thought to be to enable males to defend their territory until their eldest offspring are old enough to take over the same space in the forest.

year can be divided into hot and wet times, and hot and even wetter times. The average annual temperature in the rain forest ranges from about 68°F (20°C) at night to 86°F (30°C) during the day. An average of 9.8 in (25 cm) of rain falls every day. Most of this falls during the afternoons, in spectacular thunderstorms. During such a downpour, orangutans have been known to cover themselves

---

ORANGUTAN DENSITY VARIES BETWEEN 0.25 TO 1.25 ANIMALS PER SQUARE MILE, DEPENDING ON HABITAT QUALITY

---

with large leaves—with all that fur, getting soaking wet is no fun at all.

Orangutans wander through the rain forest, searching for food. But they do not roam completely at random. They follow well-established travel routes that, combined with their vast knowledge of the forest and the fruiting habits of the trees in it, lead them to the trees most likely to provide them with a decent meal. They also follow the movements of other animals, such as hornbills, which share their liking for fruit and can lead them to a

good source of food. Because of their bulk and weight, orangutan movements are normally slow and deliberate, and they only travel a few hundred yards a day through the trees.

When several adult orangutans meet, because they are attracted to the same food source such as a fruiting fig tree, they show no social interaction and depart separately after they have had their fill. However, orangutans do recognize other animals whose ranges they overlap, and have a good knowledge of the whereabouts of other individuals. ∎

FOCUS ON

THE JUNGLE OF BORNEO

The rain forests of Borneo are famous for their huge butterflies, gigantic trees, hanging lianas (vines), buzzing insects, and, of course, for their orangutans. Despite their huge size and brightly colored coats, they are surprisingly difficult to see among the lush foliage of the forest. A grunt or the creak of a tree branch may be all that gives them away.

Borneo is the third largest island in the world. It lies across the equator in Southeast Asia. Although its tropical rain forest is fast disappearing, patches still remain along the coasts and on the hills inland. There are also mangrove swamps along the coasts. The Bornean rain forest contains thousands of different species of tree. Among the most common are the dipterocarp trees, with their two-winged fruits.

ANNUAL RAINFALL

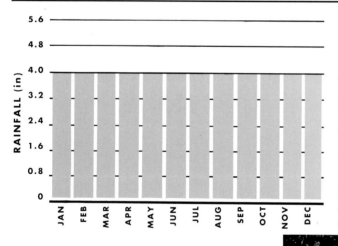

RAINFALL (in): 5.6, 4.8, 4.0, 3.2, 2.4, 1.6, 0.8, 0

JAN FEB MAR APR MAY JUN JUL AUG SEP OCT NOV DEC

There is no distinct dry season, though the least amount of rain tends to fall in July, August, and September (when areas of felled jungle are burned off). The average rainfall in most localities is about 150 inches a year, most of which falls between late afternoon and early morning.

NEIGHBORS

Orangutans have no shortage of neighbors in their forest homes, as the rain forests of the world contain at least half of all the species of plants and animals on earth.

HORNBILL

The hornbill's huge, bony casque may help to amplify its calls so that they carry through the forest.

BIRDWING BUTTERFLY

The Bornean jungle is home to birdwing butterflies, which have wingspans of up to 7.8 in.

RESERVES
Orang populations are protected in the Gunung Palung and Bukit Raja Reserves in Indonesian Kalimantan (in the southeast) and in the Lajak Entimau Reserve in Sarawak (in the northwest). A further reserve is proposed for Sabah (in the northeast).

COLUGO

Colugo, or flying lemur, has flaps of furry skin stretched between its front and back limbs.

FLYING FROG

Wallace's flying frog is able to glide by stretching out the webbing between its fingers and toes.

FLYING SNAKE

The golden flying snake is able to escape predators and pursue its prey through the trees.

CENTIPEDE

These creatures are active predators, hunting insects, spiders, worms, and other small prey.

BROWN TORTOISE

Like other species of tortoise, the brown tortoise withdraws into its shell when faced with predators.

SOCIAL STRUCTURE

For the most part, orangutans keep to themselves. Their solitary nature may be due to the fact that their favorite food of fruit is widely scattered throughout the forest. The population is forced to split up and search for food further afield. No single food source is large enough to support a large concentration of animals. The fact of the matter seems to be that orangutans cannot afford to be too sociable, for fear of starving.

Adult males are the most solitary of all orangutans. They set off on their own as soon as they leave their mother's care. Their only deliberate, but brief, encounters with other orangutans occur when males and females come together to mate. Courtship and mating last for a few days at most,

---

OVER CONDENSED ORANGUTAN POPULATIONS RESULT IN INCREASED AGGRESSION BETWEEN MALES

---

however. Then the male wanders off on his own again. He usually takes no further interest in the female or in his offspring, although he may (very rarely) stay with the female during her pregnancy.

Males move through the forest in territories of several square miles that overlap at the edges with the territories of several other orangutans. Trespassers, and accidental encounters with other orangutans, are not encouraged. Males call to identify themselves as the rightful owners of a particular patch of forest (see Insight box opposite). This is usually enough to send any other males skulking away. If they do persevere into his territory, however, the encounter often ends in a fight. Each male uses his great size, long hair, and vast cheek and throat pouches to make himself look as intimidating as possible. Fights are sometimes to the death. They are always viciously hard-fought battles. Many older males carry war wounds, such as deep scars on their faces and bitten-off or broken fingers. Some males are occasional nomads, leaving their own territories for up to two years at a time, possibly to seek out better and more fruitful sources of food in other parts of the forest. Sexually immature males, and sometimes females, may also wander on their own before establishing their own territories.

Apart from the long call of the male, orangutans are normally quiet animals. Most of the sounds they make consist of piglike grunts, hooting noises, sighs, and a strange sucking sound.

ORANGUTAN NEST BUILDING

At night, orangutans build themselves large, leafy nests in the trees of the jungle canopy, at least 33 ft (10 m) above ground. A new nest is built every night, by bending over branches into a firm base and tucking in smaller twigs to make a springy mattress. A twig roof and a scattering of soft leaves, and the bed for the night is complete. Orangutans sleep on their backs or sides, sometimes with a hand under their head, just like a sleeping human being. Young orangutans learn how to make sleeping nests at an early age, by playacting and copying their mothers. Their first attempts do not last long, but practice makes perfect.

Barry Croucher/Wildlife Art Agency

Michael K. Nichols/Magnum Photos

THE LONG CALL

Every so often, the jungle peace is shattered by the extraordinary "long call" of a male orangutan. This starts off as a series of roars that get ever louder until they reach an earsplitting bellow. The call is made deeper and more resonant by the male's great throat pouches, which he inflates with air. It lasts for 2–3 minutes, then subsides into a burbling sigh as the pouches deflate. It can be heard over half a mile away. It is thought that the call acts as a spacing mechanism in the forest, to advertise a male's presence and keep rival males out of his territory. It may also help to attract females, though this is not certain. According to local legend, the call is a cry of pain. It was made by an orangutan who returned to his nest to find that the human bride he had captured was missing.

Single female orangutans travel through the forest with one or two young, a baby, and possibly an older sister or brother, in tow. This is usually the extent of their family group, although several mothers and their offspring may sometimes collect in small "mother groups." This is the largest type of social unit in orangutan society, and only lasts for a day or two. Larger numbers of orangutans may congregate at a particularly productive fruit tree for a rare feast. But, by and large, they ignore each other's presence and simply get on with the business of eating their fill, then go their separate ways.

Young orangutans are more sociable than their parents, playing games with others of their own age whenever they meet. But they too gradually become more and more independent. By the time they are 7–10 years old, they have parted company completely with their mothers. ■

FOOD AND FEEDING

About 60 percent of an orangutan's diet consists of tropical fruit, such as mangoes, mangosteens, figs, durian fruit, rambutans, jackfruits, and litchis. Durian fruit are special favorites. These are large, spiky-skinned fruit about the same size as footballs. The orangutans do not seem in the least put off by the fruit's strong smell, a mixture of bad eggs and smelly socks. Orangutans have large, strong teeth and jaws for tearing and grinding tough plants, fruit, and nuts. They use their teeth and rubbery lips to peel fruit while gripping it with their hands or feet.

Fruit is not always widely available in the forest, however, and the orangutans have to be prepared to vary their diet when the need arises. In fact, they eat more than 300 different types of food, including leaves, bark, ants, termites, fungi, honey, lianas (woody vines), handfuls of soil (which is rich in nourishing minerals), and birds' eggs. A Sumatran orangutan was even observed feasting on a baby gibbon, although orangutans are not generally big meat-eaters.

GORGING

The exact makeup of the orangutans' daily diet depends on the season and the availability of particular types of food. Orangutans have huge appetites, as befits their great size. They will often spend a whole day sitting in the same tree, gorging themselves on the fruit. Usually, however, they have to roam far and wide in search of fruit. The different types of trees are widely scattered through the forest and have different patterns of fruiting. Some only bear fruit once every 25 years or so. Some produce fruit on a more regular basis, but only on one branch at a time. Others only come into fruit when the weather is cooler or less humid or produce fruit that ripens very quickly so has to be found and eaten quickly. This lack of a set, or consistent, pattern makes finding enough fruit to eat very hard work. But orangutans have an amazing ability to remember the location of various trees and the times at which they come into fruit. If they simply wandered through the forest at random, many of their journeys would be wasted. So routes are carefully planned to lead, in the most straightforward manner, to the most productive trees. Young orangutans learn these routes from their mothers at an early age.

The orangutans have a remarkable memory and can remember the way to various trees from one year to the next with incredible accuracy. Very occasionally, the orangutans enjoy a rare treat. A large

Barry Croucher/Wildlife Art Agency

THE DURIAN DIET
Orangutans bite the durian fruits from their stems, wrench them open, and leisurely pull out the soft, white pulp, smacking their lips as they gobble it up.

fruit tree, such as a fig tree, comes into fruit and there is plenty of food to go around. The tree attracts a large number of orangutans, males, females, and young, over the next few days. The orangutans may even build their nests in the tree so that they do not waste any opportunities for feeding.

Orangutans drink rainwater, which is available in abundance in the rain forest. They scoop water out of holes in hollow trees using their hands as cups, or sucking the drops of water off their fur.

FORAGING

The orangutan has a huge capacity for food and will sometimes spend a whole day sitting in a single fruit tree, gorging. Around 60 percent of their diet is fruit, such as durians, litchis, mangoes, and figs.

NIMBLE FINGERS

Orangutans use their strong arms to break off branches to use as tools to dislodge fruit. They also use their body weight to bend trunks and branches in the required direction.

(in) S I G H T

ZOO DIETS

In captivity, orangutans are fed twice a day, in the morning and evening. Their morning meal consists of about 4.4 lb (2 kg) of special primate pellets, together with nuts and raisins. In the evening, they feast on fruit, such as apples, oranges, and bananas, vegetables, cheese, eggs, and milk. They are also given vitamin C tablets for extra nourishment. The amount of food the orangutans eat depends on their size and whether they are suckling a baby. Large males and pregnant or nursing mothers eat about twice as much as other orangutans.

Reintroduction of captive-raised orangutans would require a period of training to recognize wild food items.

Masahiro Iijima/Ardea

LIFE CYCLE

Baby orangutans are born in their mother's sleeping nest high up in the trees. The mother bites through the umbilical cord and, like many animals, eats the placenta and membrane surrounding the baby for nourishment. Orangutans are slow-breeding animals. Gestation lasts for eight to nine months and a female normally gives birth to only one baby every four to five years. Rarely, a mother gives birth to twins. Some babies die of natural

A MALE ORANGUTAN, LIVING IN PHILADELPHIA ZOO, WAS ESTIMATED TO BE 57 YEARS OLD WHEN HE DIED IN 1977

causes, which means that a female may rear as few as three young in her lifetime.

At birth, a baby orangutan weighs about 3 lb (1.5 kg). In common with many baby animals, it has an extremely appealing appearance, with spiky hair on its head and a moonlike face. This, together with its small size and jerky movements, is designed to send out a message to other orangutans that here is a baby needing to be cared for.

All mammals feed their young on milk and show some form of parental care toward them. This care lasts for the longest time among the primates,

OUT OF ACTION

COMMON DISEASES

Like the other great apes, orangutans can carry several diseases also found in human beings. These include:
- Malaria, transmitted by mosquito bites, which causes high fever and can be fatal.
- Other infections of the blood, which cause sickness and fever.
- Viral infections, such as those that cause the common cold.
- Infections caused by parasites, such as tapeworm and ringworm.

However, injury is the main risk to animals in the wild. Fights between rival males that may result in cut faces and necks, broken, bitten-off fingers, or, in some cases, death.

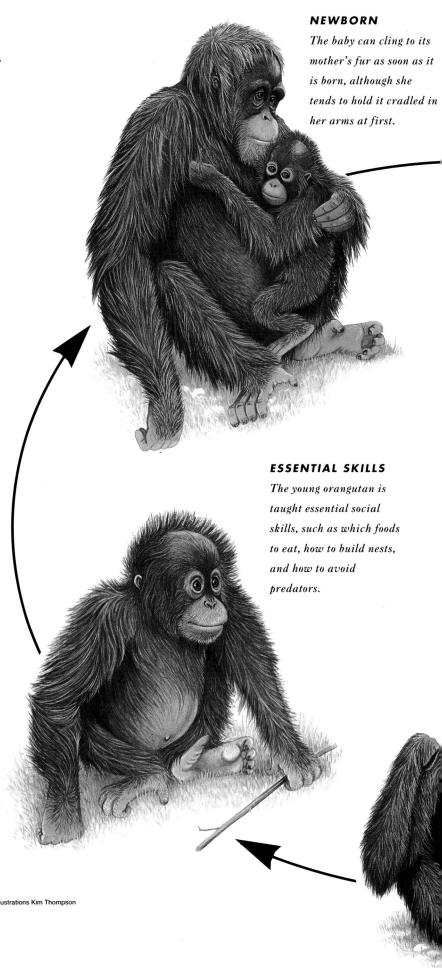

NEWBORN
The baby can cling to its mother's fur as soon as it is born, although she tends to hold it cradled in her arms at first.

ESSENTIAL SKILLS
The young orangutan is taught essential social skills, such as which foods to eat, how to build nests, and how to avoid predators.

Illustrations Kim Thompson

GROWING UP

The life of a young orangutan

PLAYTIME

Young orangutans wrestle and chase each other through the trees. This sociability declines as they get older.

AGGRESSION

Male orangutans develop the characteristic throat and cheek pouches.

FROM BIRTH TO DEATH

ORANGUTAN

BREEDING: NONSEASONAL	**INDEPENDENCE:** ABOUT 7–10 YEARS
GESTATION: 8–9 MONTHS	**SEXUAL MATURITY:** 6–8 YEARS
USUAL NUMBER OF YOUNG: 1	**FULLY GROWN:** ABOUT 6–7 YEARS FOR FEMALES
NUMBER OF YOUNG IN LIFETIME: 3–6	10–14 YEARS FOR MALES
WEIGHT AT BIRTH: 3 LB (1.5 KG)	**LONGEVITY IN WILD:** 30–40 YEARS
FIRST SOLID FOOD: 3 MONTHS	**LONGEVITY IN CAPTIVITY:** OVER 50 YEARS
WEANING: 2 YEARS	

especially among the great apes. A baby orangutan is dependent on its mother for the first three years of its life. She provides it with food, transport, and protection. It takes its first solid food at about three months and is weaned at about two years. However, it stays with its mother for several more years until it is about seven to ten years old. Both males and females reach sexual maturity between the ages of six to eight. Females are fully grown by the age of seven; males by fourteen. By the time a young orangutan reaches the age of three, its mother is probably pregnant again, and the first baby soon has a younger brother or sister to play with.

SURVIVAL SKILLS

The time spent with its mother is put to good use by the young orangutan. During this time, it learns all the skills it needs to survive on its own. These include practicing nest building using small twigs and leaves, learning to forage for food, and recognizing and avoiding would-be predators. It learns the best travel routes through the forest and the times at which the trees comes into fruit.

As male orangutans mature, they gradually develop the characteristic throat and cheek pouches of adulthood. They also grow longer hair than the females—it can reach over a yard in length on parts of the coat. Adolescence is the time for both males and females to set off on their own separate ways and to fend for themselves in the forest. In the wild, orangutans usually have a life span of some thirty to forty years.

Male and female orangutans reach sexual maturity at about six to eight years old. Mating can take place at any time of the year and is the only occasion on which adult orangutans actively seek each other's company. When the female has weaned her youngest baby and is fertile again, she seeks out a male to mate with. First, however, the two engage in a period of peaceful courtship lasting for several days or even weeks. Mating itself takes place high up in the trees. Then the two separate and return to their individual lives. ∎

DOWN BUT NOT OUT

ALTHOUGH PROTECTED BY LAW, THE ORANGUTAN IS STILL UNDER THREAT—FROM LOGGERS WHO INVADE AND DESTROY ITS HABITAT AND POACHERS WHO CAPTURE BABIES FOR THE ZOO AND PET TRADE

Fossil remains show that orangutans were once widespread in Asia. On the mainland, they ranged from India to China and as far south as Java. Today, they are restricted to small, and ever-decreasing, patches of tropical rain forest on Borneo and Sumatra. In the 1960s, it was estimated that the number of wild orangutans had dropped to an alarming low of just 4,000 animals. More recent figures suggest that, despite the very real threat to their survival, things are not as dire as they first seemed. In areas of good quality habitat, the density of orangutans may be between one and four animals per square mile. The wild orangutan population is probably now around 30,000. The threat posed to its habitat, however, continues to place this extraordinary creature at great risk.

In common with all the great apes, and many species of primates, the orangutan is officially classed as an endangered species by the IUCN (International Union for the Conservation of Nature), or the World Conservation Union. An endangered species is defined as one that is "in danger of extinction and whose survival is unlikely if the causal factors continue operating." In the case of the orangutan, the causal factors in question are the result of human activities—the most dangerous being the destruction of the orangutan's forest habitat and the illegal pet trade in baby orangutans that continues despite the efforts of both conservation groups and the governments of Indonesia and Malayasia to stamp it out.

> IN CAPTIVITY, ORANGUTANS EASILY LEARN—OR DISCOVER FOR THEMSELVES—HOW TO WALK ERECT

Since early humans first appeared in Borneo and Sumatra, people have been in competition with orangutans, sharing a liking for the same food and for the same land. There is evidence that prehistoric humans hunted and ate orangutans. This comes from the burned remains of orangutan bones found in the Niah Caves in Sarawak, which date from about 40,000 years ago. Some local tribes will still eat orangutans if there is nothing else for the pot, although they also treat orangutans and other forest animals with great respect. The Dayak people of Borneo believe that anyone who harms or ridicules an animal will be turned into stone. Sadly, not everyone shares their

Newly planted industrial timber in Borneo (right). *The demand for timber, and rare rain forest wood, must be stemmed if rare species are to survive.*

Slash-and-burn cultivation (left) *in jungle areas is threatening the survival of endemic wildlife.*

Alain Compost/Bruce Coleman Ltd.

Hans Christian Heap/Planet Earth Pictures

THEN & NOW

This map shows the main areas of orangutan habitat that are under threat from loggers.

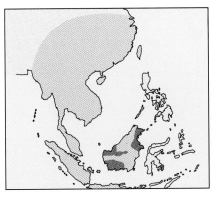

■ **PRESENT RANGE**   ▨ **FORMER RANGE**

The major threat to the future survival of the orangutan comes from the destruction of its natural habitat by commercial logging companies. Tropical hardwoods, from rain forest trees such as mahogany and teak, are extremely valuable commodities in a vast worldwide trade. The timber is shipped all over the world to be used for furniture, building, household items, and so on. Most of this wood is bought by people living in wealthy, developed countries. The biggest consumers are Japan and the United States. In 1950, some 6.5 million cubic yards of tropical hardwood was sold internationally. This had risen to 120 million cubic yards by 1980. It is expected to increase by half as much again by the end of the 20th century.

concern. In many parts of the world, ape "trophies," such as skulls and bones, are sold for obscenely high prices.

FOREST FELLING

Habitat destruction is a major threat to the orangutan. All over the world, the tropical rain forests are being felled at an alarming rate to clear space for growing populations to live in and farm, and for international companies to exploit for minerals and timber. In Southeast Asia, more and more of the forest is being cleared for agriculture. Unfortunately, these are short-term solutions to feeding a growing population. Areas of forest are cleared and the trees felled and burned. But, with no tree roots to bind the soil together, it soon becomes useless and infertile. The farmers have to move elsewhere and start again. In the meantime, it takes the forest thousands of years to return to its original state, if indeed it ever does. But it is the logging companies that are responsible for the worst of the destruction. The logging itself is devastating enough, without the attendant pressures of road building that allow easier access not only for the loggers but for hunters and poachers too. Gradually, the orangutans have been driven out of the lowland forest and into the less inviting mountainous forest regions. In short, the loggers invade the orangutans' habitat, extract its valuable timber, and leave it eroded and uninhabitable.

GRAVE CONSEQUENCES

Commercial logging in a tropical rain forest not only upsets the balance and diversity of the various tree species. The crowded, intertwined nature of the canopy means that when one huge tree comes crashing down, it brings its neighbors with it. As a result, far more trees are felled than are needed, or removed by the loggers. Furthermore, the forest floor is eroded beyond repair by heavy machinery, and the carving out of roads leads to an influx of people who slash and burn patches of forest, making regrowth virtually impossible.

LOGGED OUT

Indonesia has about 527,000 square miles of rain forest, about a tenth of the world's total. However, the pressures of commercial logging operations and clearing of forest for rubber plantations and agriculture meant that, by 1974, half of the available orangutan habitat on Sumatra had been destroyed. About half of the rain forest cover on Borneo has also been devastated by logging and road building. The lowland forests on both islands have been reduced to small isolated pockets. In the meantime, orangutans, whose home it is, are struggling for survival.

PET AND ZOO TRADE

The second most serious threat to the survival of the world's orangutans is the capture of babies for the pet or zoo trade. Although orangutans are now legally protected in Borneo and Sumatra—it is against the law to catch, sell, or kill an orangutan, and there are heavy fines to deter would-be poachers—this terrible trade continues. Mother orangutans are killed so that their babies can be snatched more easily. They are sold, via various middlemen, for export and have to endure long journeys and appalling conditions to reach their new homes. Most never make it. Only about one in every nine babies caught survives the trauma of their ordeal—a terrible price to pay.

ZEFA

ENDANGERED SPECIES

THE BABY SNATCHERS

Each year, hundreds of wild orangutans are forcibly and brutally removed from their forest homes for the illegal but extremely lucrative pet trade. Baby orangutans make popular pets among the rich and status-conscious of both their home countries and the developing countries of the world. Unfortunately, their appeal does not last long. As they get older, they become immensely strong and difficult to handle. Many are shot or simply abandoned in the street. To catch a baby orangutan, the hunters have to first kill its mother, who will not otherwise allow them near her young. The baby then has to endure a journey lasting weeks or even months, cooped up in a small crate until it reaches its destination. This may be an animal market, such as those operating in Djakarta and Taiwan (not a member of CITES), or a circus, disco, or nightclub where it spends the rest of its often short life chained to a wall, being petted and photographed by the customers. Most of the orangutans do not even survive the journey—in fact, only one in every nine survives. Over the years thousands of babies have also been captured for less reputable zoos, private collections, and for use in show business and

CONSERVATION MEASURES

Another measure being taken to protect orangutans, and many other endangered species, is captive breeding. Animals are born and bred in zoos and wildlife parks to insure the survival of their species and with the aim of, one day, reintroducing them into the wild. Many zoos all over the world, such as San Diego Zoo, Jersey Wildlife Preservation Trust on the Isle of Jersey, London Zoo, and Frankfurt Zoo, have successfully bred orangutans. This has helped to reduce the pressure on the wild populations

advertising. The trade in orangutans brings huge profits to those involved. The hunter sells the baby to a dealer who, for a large profit, sells it on to an animal trader. This person arranges to have it smuggled out of the country, complete with fake, official papers stating (wrongly) that all this is legal and aboveboard. The final customer may pay a staggering $950,000 for the baby that first changed hands for a mere $150.

Conservationists, wildlife campaigners, and customs officers have their work cut out trying to keep one step ahead of the smugglers. The International Primate Protection League (IPPL) and the Orangutan Foundation are working to expose the smugglers and look after the animals confiscated from them. They are also compiling a database of information about the people, routes, and outlets involved.

TWO STUFFED ORANGUTANS—GRAPHIC EXAMPLES OF HUMAN CRUELTY TO THIS ENDANGERED SPECIES.

as wild-caught animals are no longer in demand for zoos.

Gerald Cubitt/Bruce Coleman Ltd.

Martin Wendler/NHPA

ORANGUTAN IN DANGER

TWO CONSERVATION ORGANIZATIONS HAVE BEEN INSTRUMENTAL IN HIGHLIGHTING THE PLIGHT OF THE ORANGUTAN AND OF OTHER ENDANGERED PRIMATES. THE INTERNATIONAL PRIMATE PROTECTION LEAGUE (IPPL) WAS FOUNDED IN 1971. BASED IN THE UNITED STATES, IT USES A NETWORK OF OVERSEAS REPRESENTATIVES TO TRACK AND EXPOSE ILLEGAL TRADERS AND SMUGGLERS. THE ORANGUTAN FOUNDATION WAS FOUNDED TO HELP THE REHABILITATION OF ORANGUTANS IN BORNEO.

PONGO PYGMAEUS	ENDANGERED
PONGO PYGMAEUS ABELII	ENDANGERED

ENDANGERED MEANS THAT THE ANIMAL IS IN DANGER OF EXTINCTION AND ITS SURVIVAL IS UNLIKELY UNLESS STEPS ARE TAKEN TO SAVE IT.

One of the problems faced by conservation bodies is tracking down the orangutans in transit. They are often transported semiconscious in tiny, coffinlike boxes, which are labeled "birds" or "snakes." Some travel in secret compartments that are difficult to detect. And guilty smugglers are often let off with only a fine or a warning.

CITES

The trade in orangutans and other threatened species of wildlife is regulated by the national laws of the countries involved and by the international treaty called CITES (the Convention on International Trade in Endangered Species). This was set up in 1975 and now has over 100 signatories. The most endangered species, which include orangutans, are listed in Appendix I to the convention. All commercial trade is banned in wild-caught animals listed in the appendix.

LOOPHOLES

Despite this, however, there are many loopholes that unscrupulous traders and countries that do not belong to CITES can exploit. For example, captive-bred orangutans may be traded as if they belong to Appendix II of the convention. This allows trading to take place if the animals have the proper, official certification. Inevitably, a lucrative trade has grown up in producing fake

1559

Jann Purcell/Colorific

The Dayak and Punan people of Borneo show orangutans great respect, because they feel spiritually related to them. Keeping orangutans as pets was very popular in Malaysia and Indonesia before it was made illegal. Most made sensitive and gentle pets, although some captive males became bad-tempered and turned viciously on their keepers, sometimes even biting a finger or two off. Some Dayak hunters have reported being attacked by huge male orangutans, whom they have come upon unexpectedly on the forest floor, but this is very rare. Orangutans are far kinder to humans, their biggest enemy, than we are to them.

certificates and export permits, and passing off wild-caught animals as captive bred.

SECURITY

There is a grave concern among conservationists about the future of the orangutan. The long-term solution is to guarantee the security of the rain forests they live in. In the short term, however, stricter measures have to be taken to protect them, by clamping down harder on the pet trade and establishing national parks and reserves where the orangutans can live in peace. These have already been set up in Borneo and Sumatra and major populations of orangutans are now protected on both islands. More parks and reserves are being planned. Rehabilitation centers for orphaned orangutans, along with captive-breeding programs established in zoos around the world, are con-

---

THE ORANGUTAN CARRIES SEVERAL HUMAN DISEASES, SUCH AS MALARIA, BLOOD FEVERS, AND VIRAL INFECTIONS

---

tributing to the salvation of these amazing apes.

The rehabilitation of captive-reared apes into existing populations has had limited success and can even further threaten the wild population by spreading disease. However, Herman Rijksen, from the Institute for Forestry and Nature Research, is trying a different approach in Kalimantan. Illegally captured orangutans that have been confiscated from their mothers are quarantined for six months. They are held in

An orangutan in human company at a special reserve in Singapore (above). Despite being the most solitary of the great apes, orangutans adapt surprisingly well to human contact, as the picture below demonstrates.

groups of 10 to 15 animals so that they can develop a social structure. They are then taken as a group to a suitable area of forest where there are no longer wild populations and released. For three subsequent months, food is provided for them; after that it is hoped that the animals are capable of foraging on their own.

NEW HOPE

The success of this rehabilitation program seems to be promising—90 percent of the animals disappear into the forest within the three-month period and no longer seek human contact. The mortality rate, at least in the short term, seems to be low. ■

David Thompson/Oxford Scientific Films

INTO THE FUTURE

If the long-term future of the orangutan is to be assured, an international and effective program must be put in place to save the rain forests, its only habitat, and to stamp out the illegal wildlife trade once and for all. These things take time, however, and time is not a luxury enjoyed by endangered species. So what other ways are there of saving the orangutan?

One of the most ambitious, and controversial, conservation measures has been the setting up of "rehabilitation centers" in Borneo and Sumatra.

PREDICTION

STOP THE SMUGGLERS!

Smugglers found guilty of transporting baby orangutans are often let off with a fine or a warning. Heavier sentences will have to be imposed if this cruel and counterproductive trade is to be stopped.

These are places where abandoned or confiscated orangutans (who have been kept as pets or in private collections) and orangutans left homeless by logging operations are trained to resume their life in the wild. The majority of these orangutans will have been orphaned at a very early age by their trappers. As a result, they have not learned the skills vital for survival in the jungle, such as finding food, avoiding predators, building a nest, and so on,

PREDICTION

AN END TO THE WILDLIFE TRADE

As more and more countries become signatories to the The Convention on International Trade in Endangered Species of Wild Fauna and Flora, the trade in wild-caught orangutans will hopefully be reduced.

which other young orangutans are taught by their mothers. Many have become so used to life among human beings that they are terrified by the prospect of being alone in the forest.

Three of the main rehabilitation centers for orangutans are Camp Leakey in Tanjung, Puting Reserve in Kalimantan, Borneo, Sepilok in Sabah, Borneo, and Boorok in northwest Sumatra. ■

THE HUMAN THREAT

A common criticism of the rehabilitation programs has been that captive orangutans run the risk of spreading infections, picked up from their human "owners," to the otherwise healthy wild population when they are released into the forest. One solution is to keep them in their own reserve, where they can breed separately. Unfortunately, this is a very expensive alternative. Other critics question the good sense of allowing tourists to visit the rehabilitating orangutans. As long as their visits are controlled and limited, however, wildlife tourists bring several benefits. First, the income they generate helps conservation, and second, awareness of the animals' plight is increased.

NEW DISCOVERIES

More and more is being discovered about the subtle set of rules and social maneuvers in orangutan populations. Researchers at the Ketambe orang community found out that about ten females were the pillars of the group. They remained tolerant but aloof from one another. Infants and juveniles learned all the complicated jungle survival skills from their mothers. After seven or eight years of close contact, the bond between mother and offspring was inevitably very strong. The researchers were startled to discover that the interval between offspring could be as much as nine years, a slow rate of reproduction that has major implications for the future of orangutans.

Illustration Kim Thompson

OTTERS

RELATIONS

Otters are members of the Mustelidae, or weasel family. Other members of this family are:

WEASELS

STOAT

MINKS

BADGERS

SKUNKS

WOLVERINE

FERRETS

MARTENS

HONEY BADGER

Laurie Campbell/NHPA

ARTFUL DODGERS

OTTERS ARE WELL ADAPTED TO A WATERY LIFESTYLE, WITH THEIR GLOSSY, STREAMLINED BODIES THAT GLIDE GRACEFULLY AND ELUSIVELY THROUGH RIVER OR STREAM

A s the mist rises from the water, a telltale ripple betrays the presence of some unseen activity. In the half-light of dawn a glimpse of a creature swimming toward the bank is all that can be seen of an animal moving effortlessly through the water—an otter.

Otters are amphibious—that is, they are able to live both on land and in the water. Most species search for their food in the water, but are also at home on the land. The only members of their family

with this sort of lifestyle, otters are related to the badger, skunk, polecat, and mink. All these small to medium-sized carnivores belong to the weasel family or Mustelidae (mus-TEL-id-ie).

There has been much disagreement among zoologists about otter classification, specifically the number of species. Although the most recent classification (1991) listed 13 species, Davis's 1978 division into 9 species is still accepted by many.

Three otters—all belonging to the genus *Lutra*

CLASSIFICATION

Otters are carnivores or meat-eaters. There are two types of carnivore: the doglike forms and the catlike forms. The doglike group consists of four families, one of which is the weasel or mustelid family. This family is broken down into five subfamilies, and the otter subfamily is further subdivided into four genera containing thirteen different species.

ORDER
Carnivora
(carnivores)

SUPERFAMILY
Canoidea
(doglike forms)

FAMILY
Mustelidae
(weasels)

SUBFAMILY
Lutrinae
(otters)

GENERA
four

SPECIES
thirteen

Frans Lanting/ZEFA-Minden

Photo Researchers/ZEFA

(LOO-tra)—are sometimes classed together to form the group known as the "river otters": the Eurasian otter, the American river otter, and the sea cat. Other otters include the sea otter, with its flipperlike hind feet, and the giant otter, largest of the otters.

Otters evolved from animals that spent all their time on land. The first animal clearly recognizable as an otter lived in France about 25 million years ago. *Potamotherium* (pot-am-o-THEE-ree-um) had the sinuous body and short legs of the modern otter and a similar lifestyle, hunting fish in the water with the help of its acute sight and hearing.

Although the otter still retains the obvious shape of all members of the mustelid family, with their relatively long bodies, short legs, and thick tails, it

---

THE OTTER'S EARLIEST ANCESTORS
WERE LAND MAMMALS. AS THEY EVOLVED
THEY TOOK TO THE WATER

---

has successfully adapted to a semiaquatic lifestyle over a long period of time, and its streamlined body with its effective torpedo shape allows least resistance and maximum speed when hunting.

WEBBED FEET

The otter's webbed feet help it to swim fast. The amount of webbing possessed by each species varies, though—river and sea otters have much more than clawless and small-clawed otters.

Most otters have claws. River otters have sharp, curved claws for gripping slippery fish and climbing muddy riverbanks. Clawless otters, in contrast, have sensitive fingers, which they use to feel for

THE WARM-UP

Otters have two kinds of hair, an outer layer of long, thick guard hairs coated with oil to repel water, and a finer, dense underlayer. Air trapped between the layers provides insulation and, when the otter dives, water pressure expels some of this air, leaving a trail of bubbles rising to the surface. Out of water, the fur has a spiky appearance, as if the animal has used hair gel. It is, however, only the outer guard hairs that have been wetted—the otter's skin and underfur will remain dry.

Sea otters spend just about all their time in the water, so they need to be particularly well insulated—their fur is twice as dense as that of river otters, and their guard hairs are considerably longer.

prey in muddy water. Sea otters have very short fingers and their forepaws have tough pads for gripping slippery or spiny prey. Like leopards and other cats, sea otters have retractable claws.

KEEPING OUT THE COLD

An otter's fur is long and thick, in order to provide maximum protection from the water and the cold. Although keeping warm is one of the otter's top priorities, and a dense coat is essential to its survival, occasionally there may be times when its thick coat causes the animal to overheat. When this

Bates Littlehales/Animals Animals/Oxford Scientific Films

Sea otters (far left), *American river otters* (left), *and giant otters* (above) *all have thick, waterproof fur coats to keep them warm.*

happens, the otter exposes its paws to the air while an increased supply of blood rushes to the surface of the skin to cool it.

Otters have thick coats that help insulate them from the cold water, but they need additional help in the form of a higher metabolic rate. (In other words, they are quicker to burn up the food they eat to provide energy.)

LONG BODY, WEBBED FEET, THICK FUR, STRONG TAIL—ALL HELP THE OTTER SURVIVE IN THE WATER

The tail is another important part of the otter's life in the water, as it is used both as a rudder and propeller when the animal swims. The sea otter, which eats slow-moving prey and so does not need to swim very quickly, has the shortest tail. The giant otter's tail has a rounded base that flattens out at the end; for this reason, this otter is also known as the flat-tailed otter.

A KEEN EYE

The otter's facial features are also adapted to life underwater. Its eyes are located high up on its head and its nostrils are high on its nose so it can look around and breathe while the rest of its body is submerged. When it dives its nostrils close automatically, though its eyes remain open. Otters can see better under water than out of it, and close their eyes only when they are at rest or asleep. The otter's small ears flatten against its head when it is submerged, sealing the openings against the water.

Illustrations Barry Croucher/Wildlife Art Agency

THE OTTERS' FAMILY TREE

The Mustelidae family—also known as the mustelids—is divided into five subfamilies. The otter subfamily, the Lutrinae (loo-TREEN-ie), contains nine or more species of otter; the exact number is still the subject of debate. Some zoologists have organized these species into three tribes on the basis of three characteristics: the sounds the otter makes, the shape of a bone in the penis called the baculum, and the appearance of the male genitals.

EURASIAN OTTER
Lutra lutra (LOO-tra LOO-tra)

The Eurasian otter (also known as the common or European river otter), the American river otter, and the small sea cat (or marine otter) belong to the Lutrini (loo-TREEN-ee) tribe, known collectively as the river otters. Though the sea cat is extremely rare, as a group the river otters are probably the most numerous of the otters.

THE OTHER SPECIES IN THIS TRIBE ARE:
AMERICAN RIVER OTTER
SEA CAT

SKUNKS

BADGERS

WEASELS

SEA OTTER
Enhydra lutris (en-HIE-dra LOO-triss)

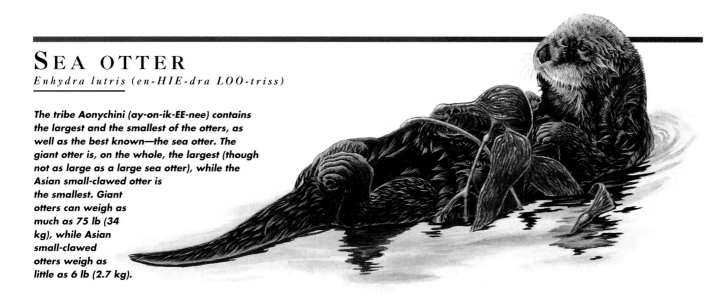

The tribe Aonychini (ay-on-ik-EE-nee) contains the largest and the smallest of the otters, as well as the best known—the sea otter. The giant otter is, on the whole, the largest (though not as large as a large sea otter), while the Asian small-clawed otter is the smallest. Giant otters can weigh as much as 75 lb (34 kg), while Asian small-clawed otters weigh as little as 6 lb (2.7 kg).

THE OTHER SPECIES IN THIS TRIBE ARE:

ASIAN SMALL-CLAWED OTTER
GIANT OTTER
AFRICAN CLAWLESS OTTER
SMOOTH-COATED OTTER

SPOTTED-NECKED OTTER
Lutra (Hydrictis) maculicollis (LOO-tra [hie-DRIK-tiss] mack-yoo-LICK-o-liss)

The Hydrictini (hie-drik-TEE-nee) tribe contains only the spotted-necked otter, a small otter that gets its name from the irregularly shaped brown patches on its light-colored throat.

OTTERS

HONEY BADGERS

ALL MUSTELIDS

ANATOMY:
THE OTTER

Otters range in size from the Asian small-clawed otter, which usually measures less than 35 in (90 cm) from head to tail, to the slightly larger Eurasian otter, to the giant otter, which can attain a length of 6 ft (1.8 m).

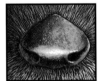

AMERICAN RIVER OTTER

EURASIAN OTTER

SEA CAT

GIANT OTTER

The hairiness of an otter's nose pad varies, becoming hairier as the otter's habitat moves nearer the equator. Nose pads range from the hairless American river otter to the very hairy giant otter.

THE GLOSSY FUR

varies in its coloring from individual to individual, while the thickness of the pelt on the whole depends on its habitat: The colder the climate, the denser the otter's coat.

THE MUZZLE

is broad, with whiskers or vibrissae (vie-BRISS-eye) on each side of the nose. These are used to detect prey in conditions of poor visibility.

RIVER OTTER

ASIAN SMALL-CLAWED OTTER

SEA OTTER

Three forepaws (left): River otters have curved claws and a large amount of webbing, while Asian small-clawed otters have narrow paws with little webbing and small claws. Sea otters have fingers that are almost fused.

X-RAY

The long body and tail and shortened legs allow the river otter to move gracefully in the water, though it walks awkwardly.

hind legs longer than front legs

baculum

torpedo-shaped body

OTTER SKELETON

OTTER BACULA

The three tribes have differently shaped bacula or penis bones. The baculum of the Lutrini tribe (top) is shaped like a hockey stick, while that of the Aonychini and Hydrictini (bottom) looks more like a baseball bat.

Tails vary in size and shape from species to species (right). The length of a sea otter's tail is about a quarter of its total body length, while for other otters it is about one-third.

SEA OTTER   RIVER OTTER   GIANT OTTER

F A C T F I L E:

THE EURASIAN OTTER

CLASSIFICATION

GENUS: *LUTRA*

SPECIES: *LUTRA*

SIZE

HEAD–BODY LENGTH/MALE: 22–28 IN (57–70 CM)

TAIL LENGTH/MALE: 14–16 IN (35–40 CM)

HEIGHT/MALE: 12 IN (30 CM)

WEIGHT/MALE: 22 LB (10 KG)

WEIGHT AT BIRTH: 2 OZ (60 G)

FEMALES ARE ABOUT 10 PERCENT SHORTER AND 25 PERCENT LIGHTER THAN MALES

COLORATION

BROWNISH GRAY TO BROWN ON THE BACK; PALER ON THE THROAT AND BELLY. CAN VARY SEASONALLY

CUBS: PALE GRAY

FEATURES

SMALL, ROUNDED EARS

STIFF WHISKERS ON FACE, THROAT, ELBOWS

HIND LEGS LONGER THAN FRONT LEGS; FEET WEBBED

MALES HAVE THICKER NECKS AND BROADER MUZZLES

THE MUSCULAR TAIL
is used for moving and steering while swimming, and as a supporting third leg when the otter stands on its hind legs.

SEA OTTER

The hind foot of the sea otter (right) is large and fully webbed. In most species, the hind foot is larger than the forefoot and the extent of the webbing is greater.

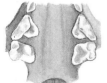

RIVER OTTER CARNASSIALS

SEA OTTER CARNASSIALS

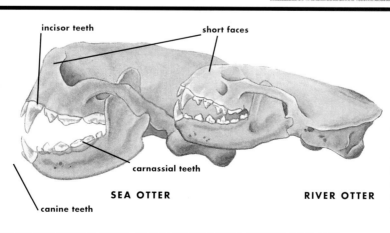

incisor teeth

short faces

carnassial teeth

canine teeth

SEA OTTER

RIVER OTTER

River otters, which use their teeth mainly for gripping fish, have sharp carnassial teeth, while sea otters, which pick up food with their paws, have bigger, blunter ones for crushing their prey.

Otter skulls are longer, broader, and flatter than those of many other carnivores, and the facial portion is relatively short.

AQUATIC HUNTERS

ACTIVE AND ALERT, BRIGHT-EYED OTTERS SPEND MOST OF THEIR WAKING HOURS IN THE WATER, SEARCHING FOR FOOD

T he image of the "playful otter" has become something of a cliché—but is it based on truth? Direct observations in the wild lead to little evidence that otters are playful. Certainly they regularly slide down steep banks covered with mud or snow, but this may simply be the easiest method of negotiating such obstacles for a short-legged animal.

LEARNING A LESSON

Most records of playful otters—excluding ones in captivity—involve juveniles who chase and wrestle with each other and play with their prey. However, as with other animals, this play reinforces social bonds and could provide them with essential training for future hunting and fighting activities. In captivity, of course, otters have time to play because they don't have to spend hours searching for food.

Otters are active animals. They have as many as four hour-long hunting sessions each day, as their rapid metabolism means that they need to eat at frequent intervals. Between foraging and eating, they spend their time on the riverbank, grooming,

> OTTERS ARE NOT NEARLY AS PLAYFUL AS THEY SEEM; SLIDING DOWN MUD BANKS IS A FAST AND PRACTICAL WAY TO TRAVEL

resting, and sleeping. Male otters tend to have longer periods of activity than females.

Otters sleep in the open as well as in dens. They may use several dens in one day. Some are permanent and are used fairly regularly, while others are temporary constructions, often hidden under a snowdrift or pile of brushwood.

Some otters, including river otters, are largely nocturnal, while others, such as the giant otter, are active during the day. Sea otters tend to be most

Resting between hectic hunting sessions, these Asian small-clawed otters (right) *are sunning themselves on a fallen tree. Unlike the solitary Eurasian, this is one of the more sociable species.*

Goetz. D. Plage/Bruce Coleman Ltd.

Dexterous hunters, such as the African clawless otter (above), *usually eat invertebrate prey, such as frogs and crabs, but will sometimes relish a meal of tasty fish.*

Tom McHugh/Photo Researchers/OSF

A male and a female American river otter (below) swim together as part of the courtship ritual. After mating, the otters will go their separate ways once more.

Franz J. Camenzind/Planet Earth Pictures

active in early morning and late evening, though sometimes they are also out and about at night.

Though on land an otter moves with a distinctive, awkward, humpbacked gait, it swims gracefully, propelling itself forward by moving its body and tail up and down and kicking its hind legs. Its forelegs are held close to its body when they are not being used for steering.

WHEN CHASING A FISH, AN OTTER DIVES INTO THE WATER, POINTING ITS HEAD DOWN AND KICKING ITS HIND LEGS

Apart from females and their cubs, river otters are largely solitary animals with little social interaction. A male and female may, however, pair up for a short time during the breeding season. In contrast, the giant otter lives in noisy groups of as many as twenty animals, consisting of several families—though between three and eight otters is the usual size. Asian small-clawed otters, African clawless otters, and spotted-necked otters are also quite sociable.

Sea otters are seen in groups of up to several hundred animals of the same sex, which are known as rafts or pods, but despite this there is little evidence of social bonding. It seems they group together because hunting grounds are limited.

SOUNDING OFF

The otter has a wide range of calls, and these vary according to species. All otters have what is known as a "contact call," which they make to let their cubs, mother, or mate know where they are. The Eurasian otter's is a one-syllable squeak, while other otters make a nasal barking sound. Different sounds are used for greeting, warning, and questioning. ∎

HABITATS

Frans Lanting/Bruce Coleman Ltd.

DISTRIBUTION

Otters are found practically all over the world, on all continents except Australia and Antarctica. The Eurasian otter is found across Europe into Asia and North Africa, the spotted-necked otter in sub-Saharan Africa, the sea otter in the north Pacific, the American river otter throughout Canada and much of the United States, and the giant otter in South America.

Tragically, however, the ranges as well as numbers of these and other otters are, on the whole, shrinking.

KEY

■ EURASIAN OTTER

■ SPOTTED-NECKED OTTER

▨ SEA OTTER

■ AMERICAN RIVER OTTER

■ GIANT OTTER

A s all otters have an aquatic lifestyle, one feature common to all permanent habitats is water. Practically all over the world, otters may be found around any watercourse, from large rivers and estuaries to small ditches, streams, and ponds. Other watery habitats, such as marshlands and reed beds, also house otters. The water must be free of pollution and able to provide the otter with a plentiful

The sea otter is often found resting afloat, wrapped up in a couple of strands of a seaweed called kelp, which it uses as an anchor to prevent drifting. These otters live off the California coast near Monterey.

THE OTTER'S MAIN HABITAT REQUIREMENT IS CLEAN WATER. IT ALSO NEEDS A PLACE THAT CAN PROVIDE SHELTER AND A RANGE OF PREY

---

supply of food throughout the year. The habitat also needs to be varied enough to provide substitute prey when the animal's main prey is not available.

Otters are found in both freshwater and salt water. Although Eurasian and American otters are known as "river otters," they are actually as much at home on the seacoast as they are in freshwater. And most of the other otters—with the exception of the sea otter and the sea cat, which live only in marine environments—often live in rivers.

CLOSE TO WATER

Otters do live in nonaquatic habitats, but only for short periods of time, as they travel from one body of water to another. Even then, they will often follow streams and brooks where these are present.

Any suitable habitat must also have a range of resting areas that are free from disturbance by other animals. In some areas, a river otter may sleep out

The Asian small-clawed otter seldom ventures into deep water.

in the open, but some sort of cover in the form of trees or bushes is usually sought. Alternatively, the otter should be able to dig a tunnel into the riverbank to construct a den; this is particularly important for the female when giving birth.

Doug Allan/Oxford Scientific Films

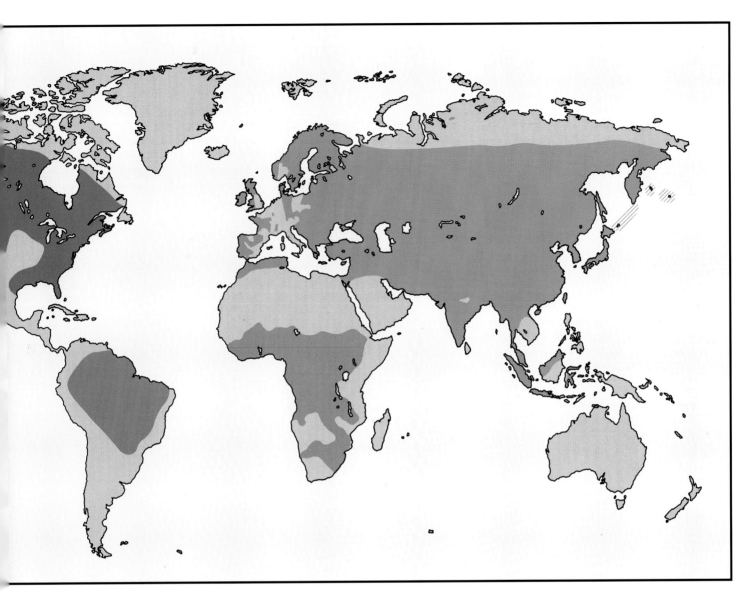

As otters have such a wide distribution around the world, being found in cold as well as warm areas, it seems that climate is one factor that doesn't seem to affect them very much. Rainfall, however, may play an important part in ensuring a constant supply of water. The main thing is that the climate isn't exceptionally harsh, as this might prevent the otters from getting enough food.

A WIDE RANGE

The Eurasian otter has the largest range of all otters, from Britain across Europe and Asia to Japan; it even reaches into a small part of North Africa. Habitats range from arctic to semidesert. It is usually found in rivers and streams of medium depth with wooded shores, and sometimes in large lakes, marshlands, or lowlands. However, when food in freshwater is scarce, it may travel from its home waters to the sea or to coastal islands.

The American river otter ranges over a large part of North America, living in a variety of habitats from lakes and streams, to irrigation ditches and salt marshes, to rocky shores. The rough waters off the western coast of South America are the only home of the sea cat. It finds shelter in caves and among dense vegetation, mainly along the shoreline.

The sea otter lives in the north Pacific, from the

KEY FACTS

● River otters will travel as far as 650 ft (200 m) from their home waters in search of food or if they are disturbed. This is usually through water, but otters may travel over land, and even over mountains, to get from one river to another.

● African clawless otters are good excavators, and can dig tunnels more than 3.3 ft (1 m) deep to use as a resting site.

● Resting sites for Eurasian otters are always close to water. In one study, 90 percent were within 33 ft (10 m) of the riverbank, and the rest were within 165 ft (50 m).

Kuril Islands north of Japan to Prince William Sound off Alaska, as well as off the California coast. During the summer months, when the water is calm, this otter may spend the whole night in seaweed fields far from shore. In the winter, when the seaweed is washed away, the otter will stay nearer land; it may rest on rocks or steep cliffs.

FOLLOW THAT FISH

The giant otter can be found throughout all the major river systems in northern and central South America. It follows its prey—slow-moving fish—into flooded forests during the rainy season then, when the waters recede, it follows the fish back to shallow creeks, streams, and lakes with low, sloping banks and good cover.

The Asian small-clawed otter and the smooth-coated otter have similar ranges: over much of southern Asia, from India eastward through China to Borneo. The smooth-coated otter prefers large rivers, mangrove swamps, and coastal areas. The Asian small-clawed otter prefers shallow estuaries

Mark Hamblin/Oxford Scientific Films

FOCUS ON

THE RIVER SHANNON

For a large part of its length, the Shannon flows through country that has never been intensively farmed. The landscape varies, from meadows and callows (meadows that flood in winter and thus remain fertile) to peat bogs and marshes. Disturbance, pollution, and habitat destruction have occurred far less frequently here than in other parts of the Eurasian otter's range in the British Isles.

Plenty of dense bank vegetation provides excellent cover for the otter's use, and there is an abundance of prey in the river, especially coarse fish, which provides a continual supply of food. This means that the Shannon, together with much of the surrounding countryside, is ideal for maintaining its large Eurasian otter population. Numbers have remained at a healthy level here, and have never shown the massive declines experienced in England.

SHANNON FOOD WEB

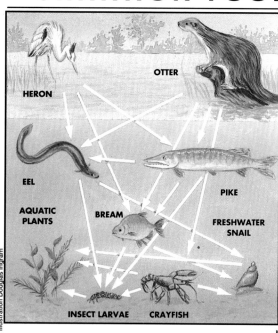

Illustration Douglas Ingram

HERON

OTTER

EEL

AQUATIC PLANTS

BREAM

PIKE

FRESHWATER SNAIL

INSECT LARVAE

CRAYFISH

Who eats whom in the River Shannon: As this food web shows, the otter has no predators but a wide range of available prey. The heron likewise sits at the top of the web. These two carnivorous predators make a meal of large fish as well as smaller prey; large fish eat smaller fish, insect larvae, and sometimes snails; crayfish also eat larvae and snails; and larvae and snails feast on a variety of aquatic plants.

and rice paddies, in highlands and along the coast.

There are two species of otter living in Africa, the clawless and the spotted-necked, and both may be found in the quiet streams, lakes, and swamps of Africa south of the Sahara.

The clawless otter can also be seen in salt water, in the ocean and in estuaries. It prefers shallow water and thick vegetation, and uses the tangled greenery for building its dens, or makes them under boulders or in rock crannies. ■

NEIGHBORS

SALMON

KESTREL

A wonderful variety of wildlife, great and small, share the otter's river habitat—from darting insects to gliding swans. They all play a part in the delicately balanced ecosystem of the river.

In order to breed, adult salmon travel from the sea to their home stream, using their sense of smell as a guide.

This small bird of prey has a distinctive method of hunting: It hovers in the air before diving down on its prey.

Illustrations Rachel Taylor

THE SHANNON

From its source in the foothills of the Cuilcagh Mountains, the longest river in the British Isles flows down through the heart of Ireland. Most of its 214 miles (345 kilometers) consists of peacefully flowing freshwater, though it meets the sea near the ancient city of Limerick.

HERON

Standing still in the water for long periods, the patient heron stabs fish and frogs with its swordlike bill.

DRAGONFLY

With a flash of color from its brilliant wings, the dragonfly flits around the river's vegetation.

WHOOPER SWAN

The whooper swan can be recognized by its yellow and black bill. Its long neck helps it to feed in deep water.

MARSH SPIDER

The marsh spider, with its eight long legs, spends most of its time on or near the surface of the water.

PIKE

With its big appetite and razor-sharp teeth, the pike lies motionless among the reeds, waiting to attack.

TERRITORY

Every animal needs an area in which to live; this area is known as a home range. The size of an animal's home range depends on how much land is needed in order to provide life's essentials: food, shelter, and access to other animals for breeding.

Territory, on the other hand, usually refers to an area—usually part of the home range—which is exclusively used and actively defended by an

---

WITHIN THEIR HOME RANGES, OTTERS HAVE FAVORED AREAS FOR RESTING, EATING, AND SCENT MARKING

---

individual or group of animals against others of the same species. This defense can take the form of fighting, but is more likely to involve a less aggressive form of behavior such as scent marking.

Eurasian otters have home ranges that they defend by scent marking. Though these ranges overlap and, therefore, are not exclusive, some zoologists have concluded that these otters are territorial because overlap occurs only at the edges.

BORDER PATROL

Males usually have larger home ranges than females and patrol them on a regular basis, covering the whole area over a period of several days; the routes of females are not so wide ranging. However, all otters leave their droppings at intervals as they go. Scented with musk, a strong-smelling jelly that is secreted by the animal's anal glands along with the feces, the droppings proclaim the identity of the otter marking the area and its ownership of the spot.

Among Eurasian otters there are varying degrees of dominance, with dominant males maintaining more or less exclusive home ranges in the most favorable areas, where they have access to several females, and subordinate males maintaining much smaller ranges in inferior areas.

OTTERS ON TOP

It isn't clear how an individual becomes dominant but, as with other animals, possession is doubtless nine-tenths of the law when animals are otherwise equal. Age and experience may also be important

SNIFFING THE GROUND

Feces and urine function as keep-off signs, and are renewed regularly to prevent invasion of territory.

WELL GROOMED

A considerable part of the otter's day is spent grooming. This is not surprising as, without well-maintained fur, an otter would soon lose its protection from the cold and wet. Certain areas, called rolling places, are used for drying and grooming when the otter comes out of the water, and these may be heavily marked with feces.

Grooming activities include, from left to right: vigorous squirming and rolling from side to side on grass or soil; rubbing and scratching; licking and nibbling.

Illustrations Neil Cox/Wildlife Art Agency

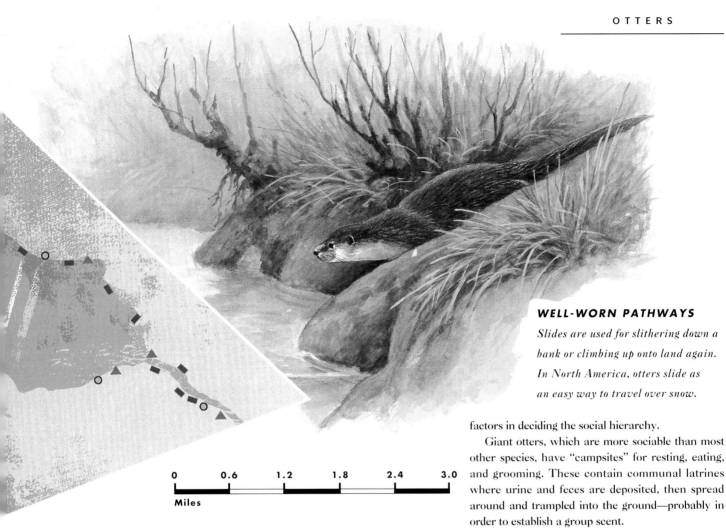

| 0 | 0.6 | 1.2 | 1.8 | 2.4 | 3.0 |

Miles

KEY

▲ ROLLING PLACE

▬ DEFECATION POINT

◉ RESTING PLACE

HOME RANGE

The diagram above shows the home range of a female Eurasian otter and her cubs, centered around a lake and its streams. It shows resting places where the otters sleep, rest, and breed; rolling places where they groom themselves; and defecation points.

WELL-WORN PATHWAYS

Slides are used for slithering down a bank or climbing up onto land again. In North America, otters slide as an easy way to travel over snow.

factors in deciding the social hierarchy.

Giant otters, which are more sociable than most other species, have "campsites" for resting, eating, and grooming. These contain communal latrines where urine and feces are deposited, then spread around and trampled into the ground—probably in order to establish a group scent.

SWIMMING AND SPLASHING

Sea otters are the only otters that do not scent mark; unlike other otters and most other mustelids, they have no scent glands under their tail. Despite this, some males are territorial, marking their home ranges by vigorous swimming and splashing, and fighting with other males who attempt to remain in their domain. The major benefit provided by holding territory seems to be to eliminate or reduce competition over the females in the vicinity. ■

in SIGHT

SPRAINTS

Spraints are otter droppings. When fresh they have a sweet, musky odor. Otters can identify individuals from their scent, which means that spraints act as an information exchange, telling other otters about the sex, age, status, and sexual receptivity of the owner, as well as how long ago the spraint was deposited. For this reason, spraints are usually left in conspicuous places, such as under bridges or on boulders. The same sites are used year after year, by generation after generation.

FOOD AND FEEDING

All otters are carnivores, but because different species tend to specialize in different types of food, they can be split into two groups.

The first group of otters (including the Eurasian and American river otters and the giant, smooth-coated and spotted-necked otters) eat mainly fish, seizing their prey in their jaws; the second (including sea, clawless, and small-clawed otters) prefer small invertebrates such as crabs and mussels, and will grab at them with their forepaws. The broad cheek teeth of this group are ideal for grinding up the tough shells.

EASY EATING

Like most other carnivores, otters are opportunistic feeders and are unwilling to turn down an easy meal. So they will eat insects such as earthworms and beetles, frogs and small aquatic birds, as well as young water voles, rabbits, beavers, and mink, if any of these prove easy to catch.

Fish-eating otters usually use sight as their main sense when hunting. But in murky water, or on a very dark night, they will use their whiskers, known as vibrissae, to detect underwater movement such as the vibrations made by a swimming fish.

ON THE LOOKOUT

An otter may wait just above the surface of the water, on the lookout for prey. As soon as it sees a fish, it pushes itself into the water and gives chase, swimming fast. Alternatively, it will look for fish as it swims on or under the surface of the water, head submerged, periodically coming up to breathe. An otter must keep within 6.5 to 10 feet (2 to 3 meters) of its prey, or it will lose track of it.

Where the water is deep enough, an otter will grab a fish from below and behind. In shallow water it may chase its prey into a corner or drive it into an inlet by slapping the water with its tail; sometimes several giant otters will do this as a group. If a fish isn't immediately caught by surprise, an otter will often attempt to tire it out, as fish can maintain high speeds for only short bursts.

A WATERY MEAL

Small fish are normally eaten while an otter is swimming on its back or treading water, though larger ones are carried onto land—either in the otter's mouth or hugged to its body with a forepaw. Usually the entire fish is eaten, though sometimes there are leftovers of very big fish.

CHASING A TROUT

Although otters like to eat trout and salmon, these are among the fastest of fish, and an otter is usually much more likely to succeed in catching slower-moving coarse fish such as eels.

AMAZING FACTS

ZEFA

TOOL USERS

Diving deep down, a sea otter will bang a stone against the edge of an abalone shell in order to dislodge it from the sea bottom. Several dives are necessary to complete this task. It then swims to the surface, holding the stone in the pouch of skin the otter has under each foreleg, and clutching the shell in its forepaws.

Clams and mussels are also eaten with the aid of a stone tool: The otter lies on its back in the water and breaks open the shell by smashing it repeatedly against a stone "anvil" on its chest.

Main illustration John Morris/Wildlife Art Agency

PREY

On the whole, fish form the bulk of most river otters' diets—as much as 95 percent of it for the Eurasian otter—but amphibians, crustaceans, insects, and small birds and mammals also appear on the menu now and then.

TROUT

FRESHWATER CRAYFISH

Illustrations Ruth Grewcock

Giant otters, whose favorite foods are characins, catfish, and perch, normally grasp their prey with their front paws and eat it headfirst, resting their elbows on the bottom in shallow water.

NIMBLE FINGERS

Invertebrate-eating otters do not have to rely on speed to catch their food, which is only slow moving—if it moves at all. But species such as the sea otter generally have to cope with searching for their prey in deeper water than the river otters. They do this by feeling with their forepaws rather than looking. When they find something they may simply pick it up and swim with it up to the surface; if it offers some resistance, such as a limpet clinging to a rock, the otter will pry it off with its teeth.

KEY FACTS

● River otters eat as much as 3.3 lb (1.5 kg) of food a day, about 12 percent of their body weight. Sea otters, on the other hand, may eat 20 lb (9.4 kg) per day—about 30 percent of their body weight—but then sea otters have higher metabolic rates than river otters.

● Sea otters usually dive down about 65 ft (20 m) in search of food, though the maximum recorded dive was 318 ft (97 m).

● It takes a sea otter an average of 35 blows with a stone to break open a mussel shell. However, one quick worker was observed to open 54 mussels in 86 minutes!

● Eurasian otters hunting in coastal areas are successful in a quarter to a third of their dives, but those looking for prey in freshwater catch prey in only one out of 14 dives.

The Asian small-clawed otter also searches for prey by touch, using its very sensitive forepaws. Similarly, the clawless otter probes into mud and crevices in its search for food.

UP AND DOWN

Otters, like all other mammals, have to breathe air and so need to return to the surface after every dive. If the water is relatively shallow, they may be able to take regular breaths while continuing the chase, but in deeper water they might need to interrupt the pursuit of their prey. Though one sea otter was recorded as staying under water for four-and-a-half minutes, dives by other species are usually much shorter—normally between fifty and ninety seconds, and even less for the Eurasian otter. ■

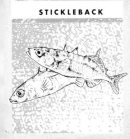

STICKLEBACK

BREAM

WATER VOLE

PERCH

EEL

COMMON FROG

LIFE CYCLE

Illustrations John Morris/Wildlife Art Agency

When a female Eurasian otter is ready to mate, she gives off signals to the male by scent marking the spraint heaps in her home range. Several males may show interest, in which case they will fight for her favors.

The winner will usually participate in vigorous and noisy courtship-swimming with the female, when the animals twist and dive around each other in the water. This may look like play but, in fact, it may serve the purpose of stimulating ovulation (egg production) in the female. Some otter pairs spend several days together, sleeping and eating as a couple, before they mate.

THE COURTING COUPLE

Mating usually takes place in the water but is also recorded on land, and normally takes between 10 and 30 minutes for the Eurasian otter. It will occur several times during the next few days, probably to make sure fertilization occurs. Mating in otters, and in other mustelids, is very vigorous; it is thought that this activity insures that the female ovulates.

Soon after mating, the two part company, but the male will occasionally return to the female after she

> **MALE OTTERS COURT THEIR CHOSEN FEMALE VIGOROUSLY, THEN WILL OFTEN VISIT HER AFTER MATING**

has given birth, occupying a nearby den or accompanying the family for a few days. The giant otter male, on the other hand, is a "good father," often staying with the female until one of them dies. When this happens, the survivor becomes distressed and completely nonaggressive.

Gestation is usually about nine weeks, but in some otter species such as the sea otter and

American river otter it can last as much as a year. This long period can be explained by a process known as delayed implantation: After mating, the fertilized egg develops slightly, then, instead of implanting itself into the uterus wall immediately, it floats around in the uterus and only implants itself and develops after a certain period of time. For otters, this allows the birth to occur in the spring, when climate and availability of prey are at their best.

BLIND AND HELPLESS

Except for the sea otter, birth always occurs on land, in a safe, undisturbed den. (Sea otters give birth in the water or, occasionally, on the beach.) The blind and toothless young are completely helpless, and their development is quite slow, even though the fat content of their mother's milk may be six times that of cow's milk. They make peeping sounds like young chicks.

Young Eurasian otters take their first wobbly steps at about seven weeks, and at the same time have their first taste of solid food. They can be seen playing outside the den from about the age of ten weeks, and in another fortnight they will have acquired their first waterproof coat and are ready to take to the water. They will not be fully weaned until they are about fourteen weeks old. After about four months they are able to catch their own food and will accompany their mother as she moves throughout her home range.

OUT AND ABOUT

Young otters are independent at seven to twelve months, when they will search for their own home range. They are sexually mature after two years.

In the wild otters are likely to die before they are mature, and few will survive beyond their eighth birthday. In captivity, however, where there is plenty of food and no dangers to face, otters tend to live much longer. ∎

COURTSHIP
Male and female swim together under the water.

INDEPENDENCE
comes at about a year old, when the youngster leaves its mother's territory to establish one of its own.

Nick Gordon/Survival Anglia

Young giant otter cubs in Guyana, South America, wait eagerly for their mother's return and the promise of food.

GROWING UP

The life of a young otter

TINY NEWBORNS

*For the first four or five weeks of life,
the feeble young suckle from their
mother every few hours.*

ROUGH AND TUMBLE

*At two months old, the young otters are
more adventurous. They spend most of their
time playing games on the riverbank.*

TESTING THE WATER

*Young otters are first brought to
the water's edge at about two
months, but will not be able to
swim for another month.*

FROM BIRTH TO DEATH

EURASIAN OTTER	SEA OTTER
GESTATION: 62–63 DAYS	**GESTATION:** 4–12 MONTHS
LITTER SIZE: USUALLY 2	**LITTER SIZE:** 1
BREEDING: NONSEASONAL	**BREEDING:** VARIABLE, MAY BE
WEIGHT AT BIRTH: 2 oz (60 G)	ONLY 4–5 MONTHS
EYES OPEN: 28–35 DAYS	**WEIGHT AT BIRTH:** 3.3–4 LB (1.5–1.8 KG)
WEANING: 7 WEEKS	**EYES OPEN:** AT BIRTH
(FULL WEANING 14 WEEKS)	**WEANING:** 1 YEAR
FIRST SWIMMING: 3 MONTHS	**FIRST SWIMMING:** ALMOST IMMEDIATELY
INDEPENDENCE: UP TO 1 YEAR;	AFTER BIRTH
REACH ADULT SIZE AT 2 YEARS	**INDEPENDENCE:** AT LEAST 1 YEAR
SEXUAL MATURITY: 2 YEARS	**SEXUAL MATURITY:** THOUGHT TO BE 3
LONGEVITY: UP TO 8 YEARS IN	YEARS FOR FEMALES, 5–6 FOR MALES
THE WILD; UP TO 12 IN CAPTIVITY	**LONGEVITY:** NOT KNOWN

in SIGHT

A BREEDING DEN

**Most otters bear their young in underground dens. The female will
choose a secluded site near a good supply of food. She will then
line the den with a variety of things, including grass, reeds, moss,
and twigs. These twigs, though not particularly comfortable to lie
on, insure a good flow of air through the nesting material and help
to keep it dry.**

**Eurasian otters prefer sites under the roots of bankside trees,
while coastal otters will use caves and piles of boulders if tree sites
are unavailable. Dens are also used by both male and female
otters as safe places to rest in. Though ordinary dens are often
marked with feces, breeding dens are not, as mothers are careful
not to give away the location of their young.**

Illustration Graham Allen/Linden Artists

TROUBLED WATERS

DESPITE ITS POPULARITY WITH THE PUBLIC, THE SHY OTTER HAS SUFFERED ITS FAIR SHARE OF PERSECUTION. WILL THE CURRENT WAVE OF CONSERVATION MEASURES PROVE TO BE TOO LITTLE AND TOO LATE?

Threats to the otter are many and varied, depending to a certain extent on the species involved and the geographical region they inhabit. However, the otter is a secretive creature that does not lend itself to research and, despite considerable interest, there is a serious lack of documentation available, particularly of the rarer species.

For example, the sea cat, which lives off the coast of Peru and Chile, has been little studied. No

---

FOR CENTURIES, THE OTTER'S THICK, WARM FUR HAS MADE IT ESPECIALLY ATTRACTIVE TO HUNTERS

---

detailed population surveys have been carried out and it is impossible to put any figures to either its decline or its present status.

The sea otter, the American river otter, and the Eurasian otter have been more common subjects of scientific study, but even then research has tended to be relatively short term, involving few animals and over quite small areas.

TERRIBLE TOLL

Otters have long been hunted for their dense, warm fur, and this has taken an inevitable toll on otter populations. The size and quality of their pelts makes giant otters especially attractive to hunters and, because they live in large social groups, they are especially vulnerable to mass killings.

As is often the case with otters, legal protection was achieved only after their numbers had been greatly reduced. Peru and other South American countries gave protection to giant otters in the early 1970s, although policing trapping is particularly difficult given the remoteness of their habitat.

For the giant otter the effect of trapping is just

one problem among many. Although the species has a large range, its habitat has been subjected to widespread destruction as forests are cleared and rivers become polluted through mining activities.

An even worse fate has befallen sea otter populations, which were taken to the brink of extinction by the fur trade. Their pelts attained prices of up to ten times the value of other fur-bearing animals such as the American river otter,

Badly managed, polluted waterways such as this Alaskan river provide a striking example of the damage inflicted on the otter's natural habitat.

Stephen Krasemann/NHPA

Ben Osbourne/Oxford Scientific Films

The map below shows the former and current range of Eurasian otter populations.

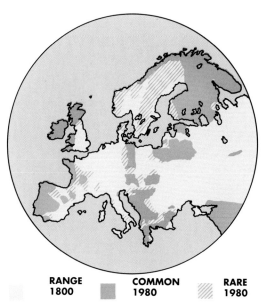

| RANGE 1800 | COMMON 1980 | RARE 1980 |

The Eurasian otter's range once extended from the west coast of Ireland to the borders of Asia, but it is now sadly depleted, especially in western Europe. Typically, agricultural and industrial pollution, along with the growth of cities and towns, has forced the species out of lowland areas up into the wild uplands.

The use of organochlorine pesticides reached its peak in Britain in the 1960s and 1970s. Usage has fallen in the 1980s, with beneficial results for the small, surviving otter populations.

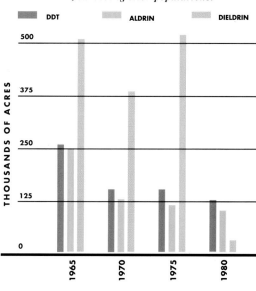

the beaver, and even the bison.

Sea otters finally achieved legal protection in 1911 under the fur seal treaty, by which time their range throughout the Pacific had been restricted to eleven small populations. Fortunately, vigorous protection, combined with research and greater public interest, has allowed numbers to recover.

In Britain it was assumed that otter-hunting for sport was a major factor in the decline of the Eurasian otter. Legal protection for Britain's otters was obtained in 1978, although many hunts had already ceased their activities. One of the reasons for the hunts' decision to withdraw voluntarily was that they were having far too many "blank" days when no otters were seen, let alone caught.

The real cause of the otter's decline lay with the

IRELAND REMAINS THE OTTER'S LAST STRONGHOLD IN EUROPE, RELATIVELY UNAFFECTED BY INDUSTRY AND INTENSIVE AGRICULTURE

---

introduction in the 1950s of a range of pesticides called organochlorines. These have a range of agricultural uses, mainly as sheep dips and for seed dressing (the treatment of seeds prior to sowing).

They soon passed into the otter's food chain. According to one source, as many as 25 of 31 British otters examined between 1963 and 1973 carried residues of toxic chemicals in their liver tissues at levels considered to be lethal. Otter numbers in Britain continued to decline until the late 1970s.

Surveys conducted in Ireland around the same time brought better news, revealing the otter to be present at 92 percent of its recorded sites. Ireland is a country where the use of the more persistent pesticides has never been widespread—a fact that provides further evidence of the direct role chemical pollution has played in the otter's decline.

NEW PROBLEMS

In the 1980s, with legislation in place and with the most persistent chemicals withdrawn, the first signs of a limited recovery were seen. But another problem was facing Britain's otters—loss of habitat.

This was caused by dredging and straightening watercourses and removing bankside trees, which are important resting and den sites. After pesticide pollution, such changes to the otter's habitat have probably been the most important cause in the British otter's decline.

Otters are fairly large animals, widely dispersed in vulnerable habitats, requiring large areas for their continued survival. The creation of nature preserves, a successful ploy for many other declining species, is

Mark Edwards/Still Pictures

ENDANGERED BY POLLUTION

A CRUDE AND DEADLY CARGO

Oil pollution, which causes immense devastation to marine life, has become an all-too-familiar news item over the last twenty-five years. Though news stories often focus on the plight of seabirds, otters are particularly vulnerable to marine pollution because their lifestyle brings them into contact with oil spilled on the beaches, as well as in the sea.

BLACK DEATH

After a major spill they may find their food supply contaminated or significantly reduced and oil may clog their fur, reducing insulation and causing death from hypothermia. As the otters make desperate attempts to groom themselves, the oil is swallowed and its poisonous aftereffect is one of the main problems facing wildlife rehabilitation centers.

On January 5, 1993, the latest in a long line of oil spills occurred along the southern shores of the Shetland Islands when the MV Braer tanker ran aground with the loss of 92,570 tons (84,000 tonnes) of crude oil.

Estimates made at the time suggested that up to a quarter of the islands' 40,000 birds were affected. The islands are also home to a colony of 1,000 otters.

The incident raised a number of

CONSERVATION MEASURES

• Many environmentalists believe that tankers should be double hulled. This means that the part of the tanker holding the oil is surrounded by another empty hull that can take the brunt of any collision, leaving the inner hull containing the oil intact.

• The International Maritime Organization, which is responsible for regulating the

questions about the seaworthiness of the world's oil tankers. Many shipping vessels sail under a "flag of convenience." This means that they are registered in countries where few questions are asked concerning the vessels' safety standards and where labor is cheap, nonunionized, and often badly trained. The *MV Braer*, for example, was registered in Liberia, a West African country currently enduring a bloody civil war. The safety record of seafaring vessels registered in Liberia (about 12.5 percent of the world's shipping) is notoriously poor.

VOLUNTEERS CLEAN AND DRY THE FUR OF AN OTTER CAUGHT UP IN THE SHETLAND SPILLAGE.

world's shipping, has recently set up a new committee to produce more stringent safety guidelines, though enforcing them will prove a more difficult task. For the moment, despite the efforts of environmental groups, shipping companies intent on maximizing their profits will continue to find the flags of such countries as Liberia and Panama all too convenient to sail under.

OTTERS IN DANGER

THE CHART BELOW SHOWS HOW, IN 1990, THE INTERNATIONAL UNION FOR THE CONSERVATION OF NATURE (IUCN), OR THE WORLD CONSERVATION UNION, CLASSIFIED THE STATUS OF THE FOLLOWING SPECIES:

EURASIAN OTTER	VULNERABLE
GIANT OTTER	VULNERABLE
SEA OTTER	VULNERABLE
SMOOTH-COATED OTTER	INSUFFICIENTLY KNOWN

VULNERABLE INDICATES THAT THE ANIMAL IS LIKELY TO MOVE INTO THE ENDANGERED CATEGORY IF THINGS CONTINUE AS THEY ARE. ENDANGERED MEANS THAT THE ANIMAL IS IN DANGER OF EXTINCTION AND ITS SURVIVAL IS UNLIKELY UNLESS STEPS ARE TAKEN TO SAVE IT. INSUFFICIENTLY KNOWN MEANS THE ANIMAL IS SUSPECTED BUT NOT DEFINITELY KNOWN TO BELONG TO ONE OF THE THREATENED ANIMAL SPECIES.

Nick Gordon/Ardea

not therefore an appropriate course of action. The only effective conservation measures that can be taken are to insure a constant flow of unpolluted river water and, equally importantly, to manage the wider environment in an "otter-friendly" way.

This will need the cooperation of farmers and landowners, as well as a more enlightened attitude from water authorities, so that habitats provide good cover, den sites, and feeding opportunities with minimal disturbance. Because otters are active both on land and in water, their chances of harm are increased significantly, as adverse effects in either environment can endanger whole populations.

RANGE OF OPTIONS

Once these problems are dealt with by effective conservation across wide areas of the countryside, it may be possible to help the otter further. This might involve the relatively simple task of building artificial dens and resting sites to encourage otters to settle in an area; or it might include the infinitely more difficult reintroduction of captive-bred otters.

The reintroduction of captive-bred animals has not been confined to the Eurasian otter. In the United States, for instance, similar work has involved the release of American river otters into

ENDANGERED · NOW · BY POLLUTION

ALONGSIDE MAN

FISHERMAN'S FRIEND

Three different species of otter live in the rice fields and irrigation channels that are widespread throughout southern and northeast India, China, and Southeast Asia: the Eurasian otter, the smooth-coated otter, and the small-clawed otter. Rice-growers tend to have mixed feelings toward them because, although the otters eat large numbers of crabs, which tend to be pests in the fields, in the process of probing for food they also uproot the growing plants.

Fishermen have no such doubts. Throughout the region there is a long tradition of domesticating otters for use in the hunting of fish. The practice is believed to have originated in China several centuries ago, but is perhaps now most common in the numerous estuaries of Bangladesh. When the men go out in their small wooden boats, they release their otters, who are trained to harass the fish into the fishermens' nets. For this, the otters are rewarded with a regular supply of fish and crustaceans.

A Bangladeshi fisherman and his team of trained otters set out in pursuit of the day's catch.

areas where they had been lost.

Here, as the creature became rare, legislation was introduced but, unlike Britain, this was enacted on an uncoordinated, state-by-state basis. In Michigan, for instance, some form of protection was achieved as early as 1925—over half a century before Britain. On the other hand, some states continued trapping until the 1980s.

COMMON ACCORD

In 1973, an agreement was reached on world trade in threatened species—the Convention on International Trade in Endangered Species (CITES)—though this did not completely forbid trade in any animal or its products except for the very rarest species.

The American river otter did not fall into this

A Guyanese Indian displays the skin of a giant otter for which he may get the equivalent of a year's wages.

category and was placed into Appendix 2, which meant that trade was controlled. Governments were, however, obliged to monitor the numbers trapped and to review the species' status regularly. At the request of the Swiss government, the otter was granted full protection in 1976.

> NO OTHER ANIMAL IS SO ACUTELY SENSITIVE TO THE POLLUTION AND MISMANAGEMENT OF THE WORLD'S WATERWAYS AS THE OTTER

The sad truth is that most otter conservation projects are carried out in a desperate bid to save a particular species from extinction. Few governments have the foresight to act before otter populations, particularly those of the Eurasian species, go into apparently terminal decline.

DISTRESS SIGNALS

In ecological terms, the otter has been compared with a miner's canary. This is because, in the past, caged canaries were taken underground by groups of working miners as a safety precaution. If the bird became distressed the miners knew that dangerous gases were present and would make their way to the surface. Similarly, the otter's acute sensitivity to both pollution and habitat loss serves as a reliable measure of the health of the world's wetlands. ∎

INTO THE FUTURE

The best way to save most otter species is to protect the conditions in which they thrive, preserving their habitat rather than reclaiming it after the real damage has been done.

This is best illustrated by the experience of Portugal and Greece, two European countries that, until recently, had healthy otter populations. When they became members of the EEC in the 1980s, attempts were made to "modernize" and "improve" much of their agricultural land.

This usually results in an increase in the use of pesticides and other chemical pollutants, something that, as experienced in much of western Europe, will only serve to hasten the otter's decline. The

PREDICTION

FUTURE CONFLICT

Despite the Exxon Valdez oil spillage, Alaskan sea otter populations are increasing at an annual rate of nearly 5 percent. This has brought calls for a resumption of the annual fur harvest, a move strongly opposed by environmental groups.

next otter survey taken in either of these two countries is almost certain to reveal a sharp decline in the numbers of otter populations, with the creature restricted to those areas where agriculture is sparse.

Perhaps the best weapon the otter has in its fight for survival is its very nature, which makes it hugely popular with the general public. The otter's cute appearance and its playful behavior make it an ideal mascot for conservation groups, as well as a regular "star" of wildlife documentaries.

THE GREATEST CHALLENGE

A number of societies concerned about the otter's survival have been founded, particularly in western Europe and North America. These groups promote field studies, provide educational materials, and even support captive-breeding schemes. Unfortunately, outside the developed world, people can rarely afford such luxuries as animal conservation, and it is there, where money is tight and public awareness is low, that the otter will face its most difficult challenges. ∎

BACK TO THE WILD

Otters that have been bred in captivity often display differences in behavior that may hinder their reintroduction into the wild. For example, they may find it difficult to mate or rear young, and they may not be alert to the dangers presented by predators or humans.

Because of such difficulties, steps have been proposed to license all national and international reintroduction programs so that they meet all of the following requirements: The introduction should take place in a suitable habitat of sufficient size and isolation; the decline of the native otter population should have been due to human actions alone; and, though the newly introduced otters should be genetically close to the native population, their introduction should not jeopardize the former's survival. This should ensure at least a sufficient degree of success in the future.

HEALTHY HABITATS

The effective management of watercourses by regional water authorities is central to the future well-being of the otter. It is ultimately their responsibility to make sure the fish stocks that make up the otter's main food supply are adequate in number and largely uncontaminated.

Off-river supplementation units—bankside ponds in which young fish are reared to supplement stocks—are an initiative recently introduced by some forward-looking authorities. These insure a general, healthy stock of fish throughout the otter's range.

Once these steps have been taken it becomes possible to retain and sometimes improve the otter's natural habitat, particularly in the case of established den sites. Because of the high cost of these measures in terms of financial and manpower resources, it is crucial that public sympathy for the otter is maintained, and that its conservation is backed up by effective legislation.

Neil Cox/Wildlife Art Agency

PANDAS

RELATIONS

Giant pandas are members of the bear family, or Ursidae. Other members of this family include:

**POLAR BEAR
GRIZZLY BEAR
BLACK BEARS
SUN BEAR
SPECTACLED BEAR
SLOTH BEAR**

Red pandas are members of the raccoon family, or Procyonidae. Other members include:

**RINGTAILS
KINKAJOU**

Colorific/Telegraph Colour Library

CLASSIFICATION

Giant pandas and red pandas, though both called pandas, are in fact members of different families. Giant pandas belong to the bear family, and red pandas to the raccoon family.

ORDER

Carnivora
(carnivores)

SUPERFAMILY

Canoidea
(doglike forms)

GIANT PANDA FAMILY

Ursidae
(all bears)

SUBFAMILY

Ailuropodinae

GENUS

Ailuropoda

SPECIES

melanoleuca

RED PANDA FAMILY

Procyonidae
(raccoons and relatives)

SUBFAMILY

Ailurinae

GENUS

Ailurus

SPECIES

fulgens

A TALE OF TWO PANDAS

THOUGH THEY SHARE THE SAME NAME, THE TWO SPECIES OF PANDA— THE FAMOUS BLACK-AND-WHITE GIANT PANDA (*ABOVE*) AND THE LESS WELL-KNOWN, SMALLER RED PANDA—ARE ONLY DISTANTLY RELATED

The giant panda was chosen in 1961 as the symbol of the World Worldlife Fund (WWF)—now the World Wide Fund For Nature—to represent the plight of endangered species across the globe. It was chosen because it is instantly recognizable, appealing, and its black-and-white image is easily reproduced in a variety of graphic media. Since its first appearance promoting the aims of the WWF, the panda has become the creature that people most often associate with nature conservation.

What is the explanation for the panda's perennial appeal? It appears cuddly, playful, and clownish, its name is short and easy to pronounce, and it is the carnivore that is least carnivorous. It has a special place in human affections because it reminds us of ourselves—it sits up to eat and holds its food in its front paws, even using a "thumb" and fingers to eat it with. Above all, the flat face—more like that of a teddy bear than any real bear—and

The red panda (above) *looks much like a raccoon, while the giant panda* (right) *looks like—and is—a chubby, black-and-white bear.*

large eye patches give it a human appearance.

Various theories have been put forward as to why the giant panda has evolved its strikingly patterned coat, but so far no one really knows. One theory was that the pattern might camouflage the animal, especially during winter against a background of snow contrasting with trees and rocks. However, this is now thought unlikely as, during the most vulnerable period of the panda's life, the white areas of the mother's and cub's coats would show up like a beacon against the darkness of the den.

Another theory was that the black patches might help the panda warm itself up in its cold habitat. It is

---

THE GIANT PANDA'S DISTINCTIVE COAT MAKES IT EASY TO IDENTIFY, BUT MAY NOT WORK VERY WELL AS CAMOUFLAGE

---

true that black surfaces absorb more heat than white ones, but they radiate more heat, too. So although a panda could warm up quickly on a sunny day, it would be at a disadvantage on a cold, cloudy day.

A CONSPICUOUS COAT

The most likely explanation for the unusual pattern is that, like the zebra, the panda uses it for communicating with members of its own species. Its bold appearance may help make these normally solitary animals conspicuous to one another in the dense bamboo forests. This could stop them from coming face-to-face with one another by accident, and enable them to avoid potential conflict. Even if

they do meet at close quarters, the clear-cut coat pattern provides a perfect means of signaling threat, with the black ears reinforcing the intimidating effect of the big black eye patches.

BEARS OR RACCOONS?

Until fairly recently, there has been little agreement among scientists as to whether giant pandas are members of the bear family or more closely related to red pandas.

The problem was that, though they look and walk like bears and have similar brains, respiratory systems, and ear bones, they also have some unbearlike characteristics, such as not hibernating and having a different color pattern. Moreover, they have several similarities to red pandas, especially in relation to their diet but also their voices, scent-marking habits, and the shape of their genitals.

EVOLUTIONARY PRESSURES

Eventually, however, experiments comparing the proteins of pandas, bears, and raccoons showed that the giant panda shares a common ancestor with bears and the red panda with raccoons.

Most scientists now believe that the similarities between the two pandas are due to similar evolutionary pressures in the same habitat working

THE PANDAS' TEARS

Martin Harvey/Wildlife Collection

A Chinese legend relates the story of how the panda acquired its black markings. Long ago, when pandas were white all over, a certain panda would play with the flocks of a much-loved shepherdess. One day a leopard attacked the panda and, when the girl tried to rescue it, she was killed. Her funeral was attended by all the other pandas, who covered their arms with ashes according to local custom. As they hugged themselves with grief, wiped the tears from their eyes, and covered their ears with their paws to block out the sounds of their sobs, the ashes stained their fur black. From that day on, all pandas have had black eyes, ears, arms, and legs.

on two animals. Thus these two carnivores came to resemble each other in the structure of their skulls and teeth, much of their digestive systems, and in the development of an enlarged "pseudothumb" because they fed on the same specialized diet, not because they are closely related.

ANCESTORS

The pandas' early evolution is a mystery, as true pandas do not appear in the fossil record until about two million years ago, when a miniature version of the present-day giant panda, known as *Ailuropoda microta* (ie-lure-o-PODE-a mie-KROTE-a), emerged. Then, about a million years ago, a panda indistinguishable from the modern species appeared. This panda had a much wider range than pandas do today, covering most of China as well as being found in northern Vietnam and in Burma. This may have been because the climate was warmer and wetter than it is today and bamboo, on which pandas depend, flourished over greater areas.

More is known about the origins of the red panda. Its early ancestor seems to have been a raccoonlike creature, *Sivanasua* (see-va-na-SOO-a), that lived about 25 to 30 million years ago. A much later ancestor, *Parailurus* (par-ay-LURE-us), was larger than the modern species; its fossils have been found in North America and Europe. ■

GIANT PANDA

Ailuropoda melanoleuca
(ie-lure-o-PODE-a
mel-an-o-LUKE-a)

Known as giant cat bears by the Chinese because of their felinelike slit eyes, giant pandas are otherwise bearlike. They do, however, have proportionately larger heads and shorter muzzles than other members of the bear family.

SUBSPECIES:

NONE

AMERICAN BLACK BEAR

SUN BEAR

SLOTH BEAR

BROWN BEAR

ASIAN BLACK BEAR

POLAR BEAR

Barry Croucher/Wildlife Art Agency

BEARS

THE PANDA'S FAMILY TREE

The classification of the giant panda has long been the subject of fierce debate by zoologists. Some believed that the anatomy and behavior of the giant panda showed it to be a member of the bear family; some considered it to belong in the raccoon family along with the red panda. Yet others preferred to put both pandas in a family of their own. For almost a hundred years the argument went on. Recently, however, sophisticated techniques have been developed that enable scientists to study genetic similarities and differences between animals. The results have satisfied the great majority of biologists that the giant panda is indeed a bear, albeit an unusual one.

RED PANDA

Ailurus fulgens
(*ie-LURE-us FULL-genz*)

With its long body, thick banded tail, pointed ears, and masked face, the red panda looks very much like the raccoon, its close relative.

SUBSPECIES:

INDIAN RED PANDA

STYAN'S PANDA

SPECTACLED BEAR

RACCOON

RACCOONS

THE BEAR THAT ISN'T A BEAR

The koala of Australia is often called a bear, but isn't one, despite a superficial resemblance in its round, fluffy ears and generally cute appearance.

Indeed, the koala doesn't belong to the main group of mammals, the placentals, whose young remain within their mother's womb until they are born at an advanced stage of development. Instead, the koala is a marsupial; its young are born in an undeveloped state and spend the first part of their life in their mother's pouch.

ANATOMY:
THE GIANT PANDA

GIANT PANDA

RED PANDA

The giant panda's shoulder height averages 35 in (90 cm) and it weighs about 245 lb (110 kg). The red panda, in contrast, is only abut 8 in (20 cm) high at the shoulder and weighs about 11 lb (5 kg).

The giant panda has excellent night vision. In the dark, the pupils of its eyes are large and round, but in bright light they are narrow slits, like those of a cat (top right). The pupils of the brown bear (bottom right) and other members of the bear family are more rounded.

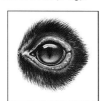

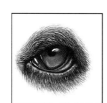

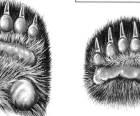

The forepaws of the giant panda (left) are larger than the hind paws. Both are covered with fur, except for a footpad and digits.

Illustrations Kim Thompson

THE PANDA'S EARS

are short and rounded. They play an important role in communication.

THEIR LEGS

are big and powerful. Pandas walk with a pigeon-toed, rolling gait. They usually walk slowly, though they are capable of running fast if the occasion demands it.

The giant panda's skeleton is very like that of other bears, although the head is extremely wide and round, and very big in relation to the rest of its body. Although it can stand on its hind legs—and frequently does so when feeding—it doesn't walk upright as other bears sometimes do.

The giant panda's "false thumb" is, in fact, a greatly enlarged wrist bone, called the radial sesamoid (RAY-dee-al SESS-a-moid). This bone does the work of a human thumb, enabling the panda to hold a bamboo stem in its forepaw and to feed with great speed.

BONES OF FOREPAW

radial sesamoid bone

X-ray illustrations Elisabeth Smith

The red panda's paws are heavily furred, even on their undersides (above). Like the giant panda, the red panda's forepaw (left) has a modified wrist bone, which is used like a thumb, though it is not as developed as that of the giant panda.

THE THICK FUR

provides insulation from the cold. It is coated with an oil, which prevents the bear from getting wet in the always-soggy bamboo forest.

CLASSIFICATION

GENUS: *AILUROPODA*

SPECIES: *MELANOLEUCA*

SIZE

HEAD–BODY LENGTH: 5–5.5 FT (1.5–1.7 M)

SHOULDER HEIGHT: 30–40 IN (80–100 CM)

TAIL LENGTH: 10 IN (25 CM)

WEIGHT: 200–285 LB (90–130 KG)

MALES ARE ABOUT 10 PERCENT HEAVIER THAN FEMALES

WEIGHT AT BIRTH: 3–3.5 OZ (90–100 G)

COLORATION

GROUND COLOR: WHITE, OFTEN WITH A DIRTY CREAMY OR YELLOWISH TINGE

MARKINGS: BLACK EARS, EYE PATCHES, MUZZLE, SHOULDERS, FORELIMBS, AND HIND LIMBS

CUBS: ALMOST BALD AT BIRTH, WITH ONLY SPARSE COAT OF WHITE HAIR GROWING FROM PINK SKIN; DARK MARKINGS GRADUALLY START TO SHOW THROUGH THICKENING WHITE FUR; BY ONE MONTH OLD, PATTERN RESEMBLES THAT OF AN ADULT

FEATURES

EYES: DARK BROWN; RELATIVELY SMALL FOR SIZE OF ANIMAL

NOSE AND LIPS: BLACK AND PROMINENT

WHISKERS: SHORT AND PALE

EARS: LARGE AND ALMOST ROUND

THE SHARP CLAWS

are used to help the panda manipulate bamboo stems and shoots, to grip the bark when climbing trees, and to strip the bark from tree trunks as a means of visual communication with other pandas.

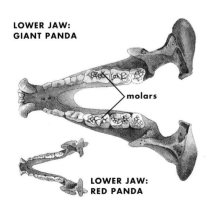

LOWER JAW: GIANT PANDA

molars

LOWER JAW: RED PANDA

Both pandas have the basic tooth pattern typical of carnivores, but modified to cope with a bamboo diet. They have lost the shearing carnassials, and the molars are broad, flattened, and have strongly ridged surfaces, enabling them to crush the toughest bamboo stems with ease. The skull's heavy bone structure allows for the attachment of massive chewing and crushing muscles.

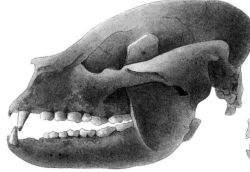

GIANT PANDA

RED PANDA

TAKING IT EASY

AMONG THE MOST SPECIALIZED OF MAMMALS, CHINA'S SOLITARY PANDAS DO LITTLE ELSE BUT EAT VAST QUANTITIES OF NUTRITIONALLY POOR BAMBOO

Like the other bears, pandas are very good climbers (right), *though their need to preserve precious energy means such activities are rare. Females may, however, climb trees to escape prospective suitors.*

Despite its popularity as a cuddly toy and its fame as the symbol of the World Wide Fund For Nature, relatively little is known about the panda's life in the wild. Although it has been studied in captivity, the information so far obtained may not be a true reflection of the panda's natural behavior.

A MAZE OF BAMBOO

Because of the giant panda's relatively inaccessible habitat, with its wet, cold climate, steep mountainsides, and dense stands of bamboo, it is extremely difficult to observe in the wild. One leading panda researcher described traveling through its habitat as "like going through a maze, or like trying to climb through the bars of a prison window." To make matters even worse, bamboo is very noisy to move through, so it is hard to watch these elusive animals behaving undisturbed.

Circumstances are so bad, in fact, that it is quite common for zoologists to spend months in panda habitat without ever catching a glimpse of the animal they are trying to study.

Martin Harvey/Wildlife Collection

> THE PANDA MUST SPEND UP TO 16 HOURS OF ITS DAY FEEDING IN ORDER TO OBTAIN ENOUGH NUTRIENTS

On average, giant pandas spend a total of about 8 hours a day sleeping and 16 hours awake, most of the latter feeding. Their bamboo diet is hard to digest and of poor quality, yielding only a slow trickle of nutrients, so they must eat frequently. But, like any animal, they can eat only so much before their gut is full. The contents of a full stomach are excreted in 5 hours, so a panda cannot afford to sleep for more than about 4 hours at a stretch, or it will stand the risk of

Red pandas (above), *less restricted by diet than giant pandas, spend much of their time in trees where they can rest, free from the attentions of predators.*

A panda leaves its mark on a giant conifer (below). *Though not territorial creatures, pandas use scent glands and claw marks to signal their presence.*

absorbing too few nutrients and starving. This is why a giant panda follows a pattern of feeding for eight hours, then sleeping for four during the day, feeding again for another eight hours and taking a second nap at night, before resuming the cycle.

Red pandas, on the other hand, with their more efficient feeding behavior, are not tied to such a strict regime, and can sleep for longer periods.

GIANT PANDAS DO NOT NEED TO SEEK OUT SHELTER—THEIR THICK FUR OFFERS ADEQUATE PROTECTION FROM THE COLD

The giant panda does not need the protection of a regular den, as its thick, oily fur helps insulate it against the cold and damp of the mountains. In addition, it will often lean against a tree or rock or curl up in a big ball on the ground. This uses as little energy as possible—and energy is precious to an animal that has such a low-nutrient diet. It also minimizes the surface area exposed to the cold air and thus helps to prevent heat escaping.

NIGHT SHELTER

Giant pandas often rest their heads on one of their paws, using it as a soft, warm pillow to provide insulation from the often freezing ground. They may also choose a sleeping site with a thick layer of pine needles on the ground for the same reason.

Red pandas use a variety of resting sites, including the top of a fallen log, a hollow tree stump, or a tuft of dead grass. A favorite sleeping place, allowing shelter from the elements, is in the fork of a tree: this prevents the panda from losing heat to the frozen ground on cold days and allows it to warm itself up quickly during fine weather. ■

HABITATS

S zechwan, home to most of the giant pandas that survive today, is the largest and most populous province in China. Over 100 million people are concentrated in the low-lying plain, which has an area about the size of France.

The name Szechwan is Chinese for "land of the clouds." It is well named, for its lowlands are bordered by a dramatic landscape of cloud-enshrouded peaks and mist-filled, steep-sided river

---

THE PANDAS ARE JUST TWO OF THE MANY RARE SPECIES THAT SURVIVE IN THE REFUGE PROVIDED BY THE MOUNTAIN FORESTS OF SZECHWAN PROVINCE

---

valleys. The mountains, which form an almost complete ring, have existed for much longer than the Himalayas, far to the west across the great Tibetan Plateau. (Although they are the mightiest mountains on earth, the Himalayas are relative newcomers, being only about 50 million years old.)

MOUNTAIN RETREAT
During the last ice age, which was at its height about 18,500 years ago, Szechwan's ring of mountains prevented the southward advance of the great glaciers. Many species once widespread across northern Eurasia before the coming of the ice

DISTRIBUTION

Today, the giant panda lives only in the mountainous bamboo forests of three adjoining provinces of south-western China—Gansu, Shanxi, and Szechwan—which form the eastern edge of the huge, high Tibetan Plateau.

The red panda shares much of the giant panda's range, but is more widely distributed. It also occurs in Yunnan Province and southeastern Tibet. Outside China, it is found in northern Myanmar (Burma), Bhutan, Sikkim, Nepal, and northern India.

KEY

■ GIANT PANDA

■ RED PANDA

C H I N A

Michael Dick/Animals Animals/Oxford Scientific Films

retreated there, surviving in the refuge created between the advancing walls of ice and the subtropical forests to the south. Others, such as pheasants, clouded leopards, and serows, were able to colonize the area once the ice sheets had retreated north with the warming of the climate, which occurred around 11 million years ago. In this way, a rich and unique mix of animals and plants came to thrive in the region.

VEGETATION ZONES
The giant panda's mountain habitat is divided into several vertical zones of vegetation, each with its own distinctive animal and plant communities. The zones are determined mainly by temperature, which drops by about 1.8°F (1°C) for every 330 feet (100 meters) increase in altitude. They are also dependent on latitude: the farther south you go, the

This red panda must remain alert to avoid the attentions of Szechwan's predators, such as weasels.

Timm Rauter/WWF/Bruce Coleman Ltd.

Liz & Keith Laidler/Wolfshead

higher up the mountain a particular zone is found.

On the lowermost slopes, below about 1.25 miles (2,000 meters), the land is cloaked with evergreen broad-leaved forest, containing trees such as oaks, birches, beeches, Chinese walnuts, maples, and poplars, though much of this has been cleared for agricultural land, which extends as high as 1.25 miles (2,000 meters) in some places. There is also, of course, a wide variety of bamboo species.

FOOD IN ABUNDANCE

At an altitude of 1.25 to 1.5 miles (2,000 to 2,600 meters) comes a mixture of broad-leaved and conifer forest. Deciduous maples, cherries, basswoods, and paper birches are mingled with coniferous evergreen spruces and hemlocks.

This is the zone of the most luxuriant bamboo growth, including the larger species, such as umbrella bamboo, that form the giant panda's main diet in spring. Away from the dense strands of bamboo, shrubs such as hazel and rhododendron grow beneath the trees, and numerous delicate

flowers and ferns flourish.

At 1.5 to 1.75 miles (2,600 to 3,000 meters) there is a zone of almost pure conifers, mainly firs, which form a dense canopy. Here, a different slender-stemmed form of bamboo, also a favorite food of

GIANT PANDAS SPEND MOST OF THEIR TIME IN FORESTS THICKLY CARPETED BY MOSS, WHERE BAMBOO GROWS IN DENSE STANDS

pandas, makes up much of the understory. It forms thick stands and allows little chance for a variety of shrubs and flowers to grow, though rhododendrons are dotted about here and there. The ground is

The dense cover of the inaccessible mountainous forests of Szechwan (inset) provides a perfect hiding place for the giant panda (above). Researchers can spend months searching the panda's habitat without a single sighting.

KEY FACTS

● **Bamboo is native to every continent except Europe and Antarctica. There are over 1,000 different species, of which 300—almost one-third of the world total—are found in China.**

● **Bamboo is the fastest-growing plant in the world. One stem in Kyoto, Japan, grew almost 4 feet (1.3 meters) in just 24 hours—an average of 2 inches (5 centimeters) an hour.**

● **Bamboo spreads so quickly and is so dense that it cuts off life-giving light to tree seedlings.**

thickly carpeted with moss and there are many fallen trees. This is where the giant and red pandas spend much of their lives.

Above the conifer zone, at up to about 2.5 miles (4,000 meters), there may be a scrub zone consisting of impenetrable rhododendron thickets, mixed with low-growing junipers and oaks.

AN UPWARD JOURNEY THROUGH THE BAMBOO FOREST'S VEGETATION ZONES REVEALS A CONSTANTLY CHANGING ARRAY OF PLANTS AND ANIMALS

Above this is the alpine meadow zone, containing rock and the small stones known as scree, interspersed with areas of grass. Covered with snow for more than six months of the year, it is transformed in spring, when a wealth of beautiful flowers bursts into bloom from the ground-hugging plants.

Finally, the tall mountaintops are forbidding,

FOCUS ON

THE BAMBOO FORESTS

The high mountain forests of Szechwan in southwestern China lie at the same latitude as subtropical Egypt or Florida, but the climate is very different. Although rainfall is not exceptionally high, the mountains are constantly damp, as clouds blanket the mountainsides.

Spring is the wettest season, though summer temperatures rarely rise above 50°F (10°C), and there are still frequent monsoon rains. Winters are long and cold, and temperatures drop well below freezing. Rivers are frozen and there is a thick blanket of snow from April to October.

The region is home to a large and unique community of animals and plants, isolated for millions of years by an almost complete ring of mountains.

Carnivores such as lynx, civets, and marten roam the forest, along with brown and black bears. Herbivores include the hardy sambar deer and three species of antelope. Rare plants, such as the gingko or maidenhair tree, are "living fossils," unchanged for 200 million years.

BAMBOO FEEDERS

fly

sambar deer

anthomiid fly

porcupine

pig

takin

bamboo rat

Illustrations Kim Thompson

Although a number of creatures feed on bamboo, few eat it in sufficient quantities to threaten the panda's supply. Mammals such as the sambar and the takin feed on leaves, while pigs, porcupines, and other animals take the more nutritious option by feeding on bamboo shoots. Sometimes the flowers and shoots are destroyed by insects such as flies, which lay their eggs in them; anthomiid (an-tho-MIE-id) fly larvae make short work of the developing shoots. The only creature apart from the panda that is a specialist bamboo feeder is the bamboo rat, which feeds on stems and roots that it drags into its underground burrows.

desolate zones of rock and ice, almost permanently covered by a thick layer of snow.

There is a marked difference in animal life as one travels upward. For example, each species of pheasant, of which there is a rich variety, is restricted to a particular altitudinal zone. As one ascends the mountains, one first encounters the golden pheasant, then the white-eared pheasant, and, in the pure conifer belt, Temminck's tragopan. In the alpine meadows and up as high as the zone of perpetual snow lives the rare Chinese monal. ∎

NEIGHBORS

Along with the two panda species, Szechwan's mountainous bamboo forests are home to a wide range of animals —the greatest diversity of species to be found in a temperate latitude.

GOLDEN MONKEY

Named for its thick, glowing mane, this attractively colored monkey feeds on fruit, buds, bark, and lichens.

CLOUDED LEOPARD

A superb climber, the clouded leopard spends most of its life in the treetops. It feeds mainly on wild boar and deer.

Illustrations Rachel Taylor

Liz & Keith Laidler/Wolfshead

Illustrations Chris Christoforou

ENEMIES

MODERATELY DANGEROUS

DHOLE
Hunting in packs, these Asian wild dogs can easily kill young pandas and have even been known to attack and eat adults.

MODERATELY DANGEROUS

LEOPARD
Now rare in panda country, the few leopards that still survive present a threat to giant panda cubs and subadults.

GOLDEN PHEASANT

This distinctive and attractive bird lives alone or in pairs in rocky mountainous areas, feeding chiefly on plants.

SEROW

An aggressive member of the goat family, the serow is a surefooted animal, moving with agility on slippery rocks.

TAKIN

This large, heavily built goat antelope has an oily, shaggy coat, which protects it from the damp atmosphere.

GRASSHOPPER

A ground-dwelling insect, the grasshopper escapes predators by using its large hind legs to leap away.

GREEN TREE VIPER

A prehensile tail enables this snake to cling tightly to tree branches. Its prey includes frogs and small mammals.

FOOD AND FEEDING

About 99 percent of the giant panda's diet consists of bamboo, without which it cannot survive. Its entire life revolves around the plant, and almost all its waking hours are spent eating it.

Of the world's 1,000 or so species of bamboo, the panda eats about 25, though in each geographical area it concentrates its attention on just a few species.

SEASONAL VARIATIONS

The panda will feed on different parts of the bamboo plant at different times of the year. It seems that it is somehow able to decide which is the best food to eat at each season, so it can extract the most nutrients from its limited diet.

The red panda is even more of a specialist when it comes to bamboo, feeding mainly on the leaves of one particular species, arrow bamboo, though unlike the giant panda it also regularly includes other food in its diet such as birds' eggs, chicks, and berries.

in SIGHT

Chris Catton/Oxford Scientific Films

BAMBOO DIEBACK

Unlike many grasses that flower annually, bamboo has a different strategy. Depending on the species, it flowers only every 30 to 120 years. All the plants of a particular species, wherever they are growing, flower at the same time and then die. Normally, the "flowering clock" of different species is set for different times, so pandas can switch from eating one species to another until the favored bamboo reestablishes itself. Occasionally, however, several species flower simultaneously, leading to grave food shortages.

A panda must eat vast quantities of bamboo just to stay alive. Thanks to its radial sesamoid bone—enlarged to form a false thumb protruding from the animal's palm—it can deal with the long bamboo stems with amazing speed and dexterity. Working together with the curved claws, the panda uses its "thumb" to hook the stems toward its mouth.

With its paws and teeth working together, the panda feeds the stems into the powerful mill of its massive jaws and grinding teeth, chewing its food only briefly before swallowing.

Red pandas have a much smaller false thumb,

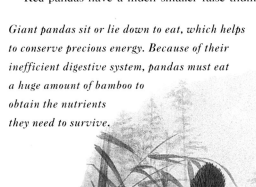

Giant pandas sit or lie down to eat, which helps to conserve precious energy. Because of their inefficient digestive system, pandas must eat a huge amount of bamboo to obtain the nutrients they need to survive.

Red pandas spend much of their time in the trees of the Szechwan forests, where they save their energy by sleeping.

Red pandas use their small false thumb to grasp bamboo leaves while sitting or standing on their hind legs.

Illustrations Barry Croucher/Wildlife Art Agency

which they do not seem to use at all when dealing with leaves growing at ground level. They chew their food much more thoroughly than do giant pandas, so that it enters their gut as a fine paste, allowing them to digest more of its nutrients.

Giant pandas still retain the short guts of their carnivorous ancestors, which are very inefficient for obtaining the maximum nutrient value of bamboo but, despite the drawbacks, they have survived on a diet of bamboo for at least two million years.

GIANT PANDAS FEED MAINLY ON BAMBOO STEMS, YOUNG SHOOTS, AND OLD LEAVES, WHILE RED PANDAS EAT YOUNG LEAVES

With their inefficient digestive systems, they can obtain enough nutrients only by eating for much of their waking lives. Their short guts allow them to deal with huge amounts of bamboo (over 10 percent of a panda's body weight each day) in a very short time, and they are lucky to have no real competitors for this unpalatable food.

A giant panda's gut is much tougher than that of most other animals, including the red panda. Its thick walls and the abundant slippery mucus it produces help protect the gut from being damaged by the sharp splinters of the broken-up bamboo stems. Fresh panda droppings are also coated with a layer of protective mucus.

Very occasionally, a giant panda will eat other food. Although ignoring other plants—more nutritious than bamboo—even though these are abundant in its habitat, many pandas have been lured to traps by cooked goat or mutton. ■

AMAZING FACTS

FAST FOOD

A giant panda eats bamboo at a prodigious rate. It can consume as much as 40 pounds (18 kilograms), accounting for several hundred stems and their leaves, in one day. One panda watched by the leading panda researcher, George Schaller, ate parts of 3,481 stems in one day.

When it is feeding on young shoots, though, a male panda can put away over 88 pounds (40 kilograms) in a single day. After a rest period of just a few hours, its high-speed digestive system insures that it will leave behind 20 to 25 large droppings in a pile.

TERRITORY

Giant pandas are solitary creatures. Males meet others of their kind only in spring during the mating season, while females are accompanied for only 18 months or so when raising their young.

Unlike many other animals, a giant panda will not fight to keep intruders of its own species out of its home range—the area in which it normally spends its entire life and finds all the food, shelter, mates, and den sites it needs for survival.

THE GIANT PANDA IS A SOLITARY ANIMAL, WITH LITTLE INTEREST IN DEFENDING ITS HOME RANGE

There are two reasons for this. First, the panda's most important resource, bamboo, is normally abundant and does not have to be defended from other creatures as, with the exception of the bamboo rat, no other animals are exclusive bamboo feeders. Second, because bamboo is poor in nutrients, after spending most of its day feeding, the panda has little time or energy left over to devote to patrolling and defending any territory.

NO COMPETITION

Despite extensive overlap in their home ranges and a shared diet of bamboo, there is little or no competition between giant and red pandas, as they focus their feeding on different parts of the plant.

A male giant panda's home range usually overlaps with those of several other male neighbors and with those of three or four females. Home ranges are located in the best possible areas for food and shelter—with gently sloping rather than steep ground (the latter would waste precious energy) and good nesting sites.

Giant pandas use scent marking to leave messages. This is the species' main means of communication and is of particular

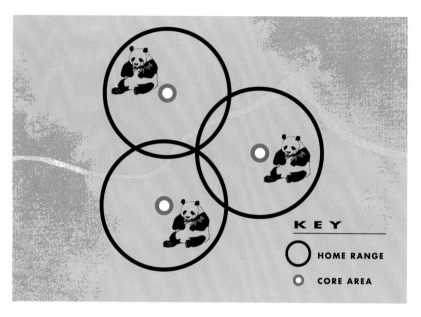

KEY

⬭ **HOME RANGE**

◉ **CORE AREA**

importance to males during the mating season. Face-to-face encounters are relatively rare in panda society and they are not usually aggressive. Even males competing for mates avoid fights and the risk of injury.

Lacking mobile ears, an expressive face, a long tail, and erectile fur, giant pandas must rely on body posture to communicate their intentions, accentuated by their striking black-and-white markings.

To signal threat, a panda will face its rival and stare at it, with its head lowered so that the black

Female pandas spend most of their time in a small core area within their own home range. In a typical month, they will visit as little as 10 percent of their range.

THE DOMINANT MALE

on the left signals his superiority by staring at his rival with head lowered and black ears standing out. The younger panda drops his head between his shoulders to signify submission.

SCENT MARKING

is the panda's way of leaving messages. Beneath its short tail is a patch of skin, richly supplied with scent glands, which is usually rubbed against the ground.

Illustrations Toni Hargreaves

ears stand out against the white fur of the shoulders, echoing the big black eye patches. To escalate the threat, the animal may bob its head up and down. If this fails to deter its opponent, it may swat at the other panda with its forepaw.

SUBMISSIVE BEHAVIOR

To convey submission, the panda minimizes the striking pattern of the ears and eyes by turning its head away. It may imitate a youngster and roll on its back as if inviting the opponent to play rather than attack. During mating, the female adopts the ultimate submissive posture by resting the top of her head on the ground. ∎

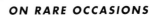

ON RARE OCCASIONS

a panda will scent mark by walking backward up a tree until it performs a handstand. It then rubs its glands against the bark of the tree, leaving a mark some 3.3 feet (1 meter) above the ground.

KEY FACTS

● Giant pandas have a wide range of vocal calls—eleven have so far been identified—which range from snorts and huffs that signal distress, to barks and yips that usually indicate excitement.

● Male pandas exploit up to 50 percent of their territory in winter. Traditionally, this is the run-up to the breeding season, when males are keeping a check on any prospective mates.

LIFE CYCLE

G iant panda courtship is a fragile endeavor fraught with difficulties. To mate, the couple have to be responsive to each other, and must engage in a long sequence of vocal and scent communication. Even then, a male may suddenly become agitated or indifferent and the female may simply have a change of mind.

The mating season over most of the panda's range is between mid-March and mid-May. Female pandas come into heat only once a year for about 12

PANDAS HAVE LITTLE TIME TO MATE SUCCESSFULLY—SOMETIMES THE FEMALE IS FERTILE FOR ONLY TWO DAYS EACH YEAR

to 25 days, with a peak of 2 to 7 days: this is the only opportunity for a pair to mate.

To mate, the female stands on all fours with her head lowered, and indicates her readiness to mate by crouching and presenting her rump to the male. The male stands behind her and mounts her, resting his forepaws on her back. Though most adult males manage to mate during a mating season, not all father young since they may mate before or after the female has ovulated.

THE TIME IS RIGHT

Giant panda cubs are born in August and September, though the gestation period varies from three to five-and-a-half months, due to a delayed implantation of the embryo. This strategy evolved in mammals living in places where there is seasonal food scarcity, so they can delay giving birth until conditions are most suitable for rearing their young.

Once she is pregnant, a female giant panda sets

AMAZING FACTS

SMALLEST YOUNG

Proportionately, giant pandas have the smallest young of any placental mammal—about the size of a small rat—and, at 3 to 3.5 ounces (90 to 100 grams), are only about one nine-hundredth of their mother's weight. Newborn giant panda cubs are completely helpless at birth: blind, toothless, pink, and naked, except for a sparse covering of white hair.

THE FIRST MONTH
of the young panda's life is spent being nursed by its mother in the safety of her den.

PANDA MATING
is brief: females are fertile for only a few days.

Ilustrations Toni Hargreaves

GROWING UP

The life of a young giant panda

AFTER SIX MONTHS,

the cub can walk and climb on its mother's back. At this time, it begins to eat bamboo.

AT EIGHTEEN MONTHS,

the young panda is left to fend for itself as winter approaches.

BY THIS TIME,

the panda has perfected the art of climbing trees.

FROM BIRTH TO DEATH	
GIANT PANDA	**RED PANDA**
GESTATION: 125–150 DAYS	**GESTATION:** 90–145 DAYS
LITTER SIZE: SOMETIMES 1, USUALLY 2, OCCASIONALLY 3	**LITTER SIZE:** 1–4; ONLY 2 ARE USUALLY REARED FROM THE LITTER
BREEDING: SEASONAL; BETWEEN MARCH AND MAY	**BREEDING:** MATING IS NON-SEASONAL
WEIGHT AT BIRTH: 3–3.5 OZ (90–100 G)	**WEIGHT AT BIRTH:** 4–4.5 OZ (110–130 G)
EYES OPEN: ABOUT 7 WEEKS	**EYES OPEN:** ABOUT 18 DAYS
FIRST WALKING: 3 MONTHS	**FIRST WALKING:** 2–3 DAYS
WEANING: 9 MONTHS	**WEANING:** 6–8 MONTHS
SEXUAL MATURITY: BETWEEN 5 AND 7 YEARS	**SEXUAL MATURITY:** BETWEEN 18 AND 20 MONTHS
LONGEVITY: UNKNOWN IN THE WILD; UP TO 30 YEARS IN CAPTIVITY	**LONGEVITY:** UNKNOWN IN THE WILD; UP TO 14 YEARS IN CAPTIVITY

about finding a suitable site to give birth. This can be in a hollow at the base of a tree, in a dense thicket of bamboo, or in a cave that she lines with wood chips, bamboo stems, rhododendron branches, or saplings to keep out the cold and damp.

Twins are usual, but normally only one cub will survive. Newborn pandas are often invisible, hidden under their mother's forepaw or tucked under her chin. In their first few days, cubs will suckle from 6 to 12 times a day for up to 30 minutes at a time.

HOME PROTECTION

Apart from its long tail, which will remain about the same size as it grows, the cub resembles a miniature adult by the time it is about three weeks old. After six months, it has all its teeth except for its molars. About two to three months later, during the spring, the panda is fully weaned. However, it still needs the protection of the nest and of its mother because of the danger from predators and because it has not yet learned how to interact with adults.

The mother remains with her cub throughout the spring breeding season into summer and autumn before the cub finally sets off to fend for itself. Estrus does not occur at this time. ■

 # OUT OF ACTION

THE THREAT OF PARASITES

Parasites pose a serious problem to the small, fragmented giant panda populations. Roundworms are most common and can be present in such numbers that they fill the animal's intestines, making holes in the gut wall. In some areas up to 70 percent of pandas are thought to be affected, suffering retarded growth, low fertility, and, in some cases, death.

PLIGHT OF THE PANDA

THE TOY-SHOP IMAGE OF THE GIANT PANDA IS FAMILIAR THROUGHOUT THE WORLD, YET, IN REALITY, THE ANIMAL IS AN ELUSIVE RARITY LIVING IN THE SHADOW OF EXTINCTION

T he giant panda has always been rare—or, at any rate, uncommon. Two thousand years ago it was the most prized of several rare animals kept in the pleasure gardens of the Chinese emperors; it was even regarded as semidivine. Such status is rarely acquired by a native wild animal, so, even though historical records show that it was more widespread at that time, it must have been scarce even then.

As a carnivore turned vegetarian, with a specialized, apparently unreliable diet that it seems ill-equipped to deal with, the giant panda looks like a prime candidate for extinction.

DISASTROUS CHANGES

Perhaps it is simply a survivor from another era, struggling in vain to adapt to a changed world. However, the environmental changes that threaten the panda are not the slow shifts of nature but the rapid changes brought about by humans, which have forced much of the world's wildlife into remote areas. This can be disastrous for the panda because the number of individuals in each refuge area may

---

THE ENVIRONMENTAL CHANGES THREATENING THE GIANT PANDA HAVE BEEN BROUGHT ABOUT BY HUMANS

---

be insufficient to sustain a healthy population.

At the end of the last ice age, some 12,000 years ago, both the giant and red pandas were widespread in the lowlands of eastern Asia, mainly because the cool climate favored temperate bamboo forest. As the climate became milder, the lowlands gradually became shrouded in a much denser tree cover, and conditions in the cooler uplands became ideal. So the pandas moved into the mountains that lie on the fringes of the icy Tibetan Plateau.

Such movements are part of the natural ebb and

flow of life on earth, and during their history the pandas had probably moved up and down the mountain slopes several times in response to climatic changes. But this time there was to be no moving back, for within a few thousand years the lowland forests had begun to disappear under the axes of human-farmers.

Until relatively recently this was of little importance to the pandas as the climate remained stable, the bamboo flourished and, thanks to the steepness of the terrain, the pandas were not troubled by human interference. Even the dieback of the bamboo—where the bamboo flowers and then dies—was little more than an inconvenience, since the pandas could migrate to feed on other bamboos with a different flowering cycle.

Indeed, it is likely that such movements are essential to the long-term health of panda populations. Pandas—giant pandas in particular—

Liz & Keith Laidler/Ardea

Stuart Chapman/WWF International

Human interference in the form of logging results in loss of forest habitat for pandas. Even in remote areas, pandas fall victim to hunters' snares (inset).

The map below shows the former and current range of the giant panda.

CHINA

///// **FORMER RANGE**   ■ **CURRENT RANGE**

rarely move far from familiar terrain, so the occasional bamboo crisis probably helps prevent inbreeding by dispersing close relatives. Unfortunately this has now become almost impossible.

For centuries the mountain retreats of the giant and red pandas have protruded like islands from a sea of farmland. But because the islands were large, with lush foothills and well-wooded valleys linking the mountain ridges, the pandas were able to range freely over large areas to interbreed and find food.

THE RISING TIDE

Over the last hundred years, however, the tide of agriculture has been gradually creeping up the foothills and flooding the valleys. Farmers grow wheat, potatoes, and turnips, cut timber for building and fuel, and graze sheep, goats, cattle, and yaks on the mountain grasslands.

All this is bad news for pandas. Restricted to pockets of prime habitat and unwilling to cross the cold, high-altitude ridges to reach new feeding areas, the pandas are now discouraged from crossing the farmland in the valleys as well. This has also denied pandas access to the bamboo species growing at lower levels, though most of the low-level forest has now disappeared. With no alternative food source in the event of a mass dieback, and no scope for migration, pandas are trapped.

When the high-level bamboo in the Wanglang Panda Reserve flowered and died in 1974, most of the 196 giant pandas in the reserve starved to death. Over the next three years, researchers found 138 dead pandas in the mountains, and today the reserve holds a population of less than 20. For genetic reasons this is hopelessly inadequate for breeding, so, barring dramatic action, the Wanglang panda population is doomed.

UNDER THE AX

Even terrain that is unsuitable for agriculture or grazing is not safe. China as a whole is seriously short of timber for construction, so the forests of panda country are a valuable resource. In theory the forestry departments aim to conserve them by selective extraction and replanting, but in practice the logging teams often resort to clear-felling. This is disastrous for the bamboo that flourishes in the moist shade of the forest trees; the bamboo that sprouts in the clear-felled areas usually dies.

The timber is also taken piecemeal by local farmers and, though each farmer takes very little, the cumulative effect is dramatic: satellite images of vegetation types in giant panda country dating from 1975 to 1983 indicate that roughly half the forest, in the most accessible terrain, was disturbed or felled

CAPTIVE BREEDING

The captive breeding of pandas has appeared to be fraught with difficulties. In the 1960s, efforts to breed London Zoo's Chi Chi received a great deal of press when a male from Moscow arrived for mating but to no avail. Likewise, the National Zoo in Washington, D.C., received a great deal of attention when their pair of pandas produced no surviving offspring. However, it is now known that breeding programs with only two animals of any species have many strikes against them. Despite this, three zoos outside of China have been successful, and viable cubs have been produced from single pairs in Tokyo, Madrid, and Mexico City. Meanwhile, the zoos in China have begun to work together to put unpaired animals together and solve other technical problems. As many as eleven cubs are born every year in China. Also, China has begun to work with other countries, including the United States, to establish satellite breeding programs. While the reproductive rate is still low, good science and increased cooperation will go a long way toward establishing a self-sustaining captive population.

ENDANGERED ENVIRONMENT

Cary Wolinsky/Colorific/Telegraph Colour Library

POPULATION GROWTH IN CHINA

Throughout most of China, wildlife is in retreat from a vast human population of over a billion. The area of land required to house so many people and the farming needed to feed them is considerable. Since most of eastern China has been under cultivation for thousands of years, the main pressure for land development is felt in the mountains and forests of the west: panda country.

A MIXED REACTION

As China's resources are limited, the Chinese government has made population control a major priority, and encourages one-child families by using financial incentives.

This policy has been fairly successful in urban areas, but has proved less effective in rural areas where many hands make light work. Resistance is particularly strong among ethnic minorities—they are afraid of being swamped by the Han Chinese, who form the bulk of the population. Since separatism among the minorities is a recurring problem, the policy is not enforced and the population in these regions is still growing rapidly.

CONSERVATION MEASURES

● Legislation implemented by the Chinese government seems to have had some success in reducing the population, though it is still growing. The problem of displaced wildlife is yet to be successfully addressed.

● Under its population control policy, the government encourages one-child families by considerably reducing the amount of benefits

.. The people who live in or near the mountain refuges of the giant panda come into this category: human encroachment here impedes plans for extending the reserves and relocating people outside the most sensitive areas.

At the Tangjiahe Reserve, however, some 300 people—60 households—have been resettled outside the reserve, rehoused, and compensated for the loss of agricultural and forestry resources. And there is evidence that, even among the minorities, the drive to reduce the population growth is having some impact. So although the wildlife is retreating, it is not beaten yet.

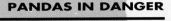

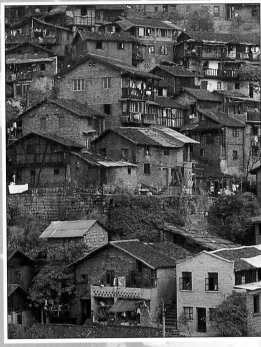

MASS OVERCROWDING AT CHONGQING, SZECHWAN, MEANS LESS ROOM FOR LOCAL WILDLIFE.

a family receives if a second child is born. If a couple have three or more children, they do not qualify for benefits at all.

● In 1984 a plan to move 2,000 of the minority Chiang people out of the heart of the Wolong Reserve came to nothing because of local resistance coupled with government sensitivity over the minorities issue.

PANDAS IN DANGER

THE CHART BELOW SHOWS HOW THE INTERNATIONAL UNION FOR THE CONSERVATION OF NATURE (IUCN), OR THE WORLD CONSERVATION UNION, CLASSIFIES THE STATUS OF PANDAS:

GIANT PANDA	ENDANGERED
RED PANDA	INSUFFICIENTLY KNOWN

ENDANGERED MEANS THAT THE ANIMAL IS IN DANGER OF EXTINCTION AND ITS SURVIVAL IS UNLIKELY UNLESS STEPS ARE TAKEN TO SAVE IT. INSUFFICIENTLY KNOWN INDICATES THAT THERE IS NOT ENOUGH INFORMATION ON NUMBERS IN THE WILD FOR THE IUCN TO CLASSIFY THE ANIMAL.

K. Goebel/ZEFA

during that period, and the process continues.

Many local farmers also hunt musk deer—so called because of the pouch of oily musk carried by the male. Musk is used as a base for traditional medicines and high-class perfumes, and to a perfumer it is worth at least three times its weight in gold. So the hill farmers set snares to catch the deer—in defiance of the law—and all too often they catch and kill giant pandas instead.

THE GIANT PANDA'S RARITY HAS CREATED A GREAT DEMAND FOR ITS FUR, EVEN THOUGH IT IS OF POOR QUALITY

Until recently the pandas themselves were of little interest to hunters: Chinese medicine had no use for any part of a panda and the fur is of poor quality. But the rarity of the giant panda has created a demand for its pelt, particularly in Japan, where the illegal street value of a single skin is sometimes several thousand dollars.

To a Chinese hill farmer, with an annual income of about $140, even a small percentage of that street value is a colossal sum. Though trading in pandas or their skins incurs a prison sentence of ten years or more—sometimes even life imprisonment or death— the trade continues. In recent years the Chinese authorities have recovered over 140 illegal skins.

In 1949 the giant panda was declared a "national treasure," and in 1957 several reserves were planned. There are now 13 of these in the mountains of Szechwan, Gansu, and Shanxi Provinces, but all except three cover less than 195 square miles (500 square kilometers). The largest, Wolong, extends over 770 square miles (2,000 square

Forest Anderson/Gamma/Frank Spooner Pictures

ALONGSIDE MAN

PANDAS IN ZOOS

The first panda seen alive in the West was a red panda acquired by the London Zoo in 1869, but zoo visitors had to wait another 67 years to see a live giant panda—the juvenile Su Lin, captured in the wild in 1936 and exhibited at the Chicago Zoo. Today there are some 120 giant pandas in several zoos around the world, including China, plus several hundred red pandas.

As long as they are kept supplied with the right type of bamboo, giant pandas are not particularly difficult to maintain in captivity—but breeding them has been another matter. Beijing has had the most success with captive breeding, with a number of survivors to date. Increased attention to biology and breeding management is overcoming the dual problems of low birthrate and high neonatal mortality.

Rex Features

kilometers), but at least half this is rock, snow, and ice, and roughly a quarter of the potential panda habitat had been cleared for agriculture before the reserve was set up in 1975. The reserves hold roughly half the world population of 700 to 1,000.

In the first ten years that Wolong Reserve was set up, however, at least 6 square miles (14 square kilometers) of forest were destroyed by the 3,000-strong human population, and poaching also takes its toll.

The reserves are also the main strongholds of the red panda in China—not being a "national treasure," it does not qualify for reserves of its own. Its range is greater than that of the giant panda, though, extending into the foothills of the Himalayas. In the 1970s Nepal established a chain of national parks along its northern mountain border, but no one knows how many red pandas these contain.

In the early 1980s, the World Wide Fund For Nature (WWF) initiated intensive research into the biology, behavior, and conservation of the giant panda and proposed a detailed management plan, recommending a coordinated captive-breeding program and a habitat conservation plan.

The WWF management plan would like to see a panda breeding program controlled from within China, involving animals kept all over the world. The researchers are confident that this would

---

THE LARGEST RESERVE, WOLONG HAS BETWEEN 140 AND 150 GIANT PANDAS, WHICH IS THREE TIMES THE AVERAGE

---

greatly improve the breeding success rate, enabling captive-bred animals to be released into the wild. The releases would have to be carefully planned and monitored to insure the successful integration of the animals, but they might work.

However, many zoologists would prefer the money was used for preserving the panda's natural habitat, arguing that if the problems of inbreeding and food shortage could be solved, the pandas could manage their breeding themselves.

A PROPOSAL

The WWF plan recognizes this, and proposes expanding the reserves to cover nearly all the remaining habitat of wild pandas, thereby linking them in order to encourage panda movement. This would enable the animals to switch to alternative bamboos in the event of a dieback, and interbreed with pandas from different populations.

The plan also involves enforcing bans on hunting, limiting forestry, and, ultimately, excluding local farmers to allow the natural vegetation on the lower slopes to regenerate. Such proposals are going to be difficult to implement, but essential. For there can be no doubt that the main enemy of the panda is human—remove human activity, and there is more space for pandas. ■

A five-month-old giant panda cub being bottle-fed at Wolong breeding station in the Szechwan Province.

Sophy & Michael Day/Bruce Coleman Ltd.

INTO THE FUTURE

Unless drastic action is taken—such as the full implementation of the WWF habitat conservation plan—the future for the panda looks bleak. The reason is a simple matter of statistics.

Biologists have long recognized that genetic variety is essential to health. In large populations of animals the breeding pairs invariably stem from completely different "families," which ensures that the genes inherited by their offspring are a broad

PREDICTION

EXTENSION PLANS

There are plans to link the Wolong Reserve with the Fengtongzhai, Huangshuihe, and Anzihe Reserves, which will create a further 1 million acres (425,000 hectares) of protected panda habitat. This will also bring isolated populations together.

sample. In small populations breeding pairs are often genetically very similar. This tends to exaggerate any genetic defects so that the offspring suffer from problems such as albinism, deafness, and skeletal malformations.

A related problem is the loss, over generations, of genes that enable adaptation to environmental changes. Such genes are often inherited by only 1 percent of the population, so if there are, say, only 80 animals, the genes may vanish forever. To avoid such breeding problems, any population must number at least 500 individuals. This is known as the minimum viable population, or MVP.

The giant panda lives in several isolated populations, none of which approaches the MVP figure of 500. Some are much smaller and these will inevitably become extinct. The only hope for the species is to link them up before it is too late. And that will involve drastic action, such as translocation to a new territory. ■

RACE RELATIONS

Since the last ice age, around 12,000 years ago, the range of the red panda has been split in two by the broad valley of the Brahmaputra River. As a result, the red panda has developed into two genetically distinct races.

Like the giant panda, the red panda is at risk from inbreeding, both in the wild and in captivity, where isolated populations are not varied enough genetically. One solution might be to breed the Himalayan race with the Chinese race. This would certainly improve the survival prospects of the species as a whole, but it would merge the two races, or subspecies, into one. Although conservationists prefer to avoid this kind of action, the merging of subspecies often does occur naturally.

BAMBOO CORRIDORS

One way to move pandas between isolated populations is by translocation—that is, catching a panda, transporting it to a new area, and releasing it. Unfortunately pandas rely on knowing their home territory, so when this was tried in 1984, the animal simply walked home, a distance of about 6 miles (10 kilometers). A second panda was taken farther away, but she became disoriented and fell off a cliff.

Another solution might be to plant human-made "corridors" of trees and bamboo between isolated patches of panda habitat. The pandas can then travel between bamboo forests when they suffer a food shortage and can feed on bamboo on the way. Fifteen of these corridors have been proposed and, if the plans are acted upon, they may prove the salvation of the species.

Illustration Steve Kingston

PIGS

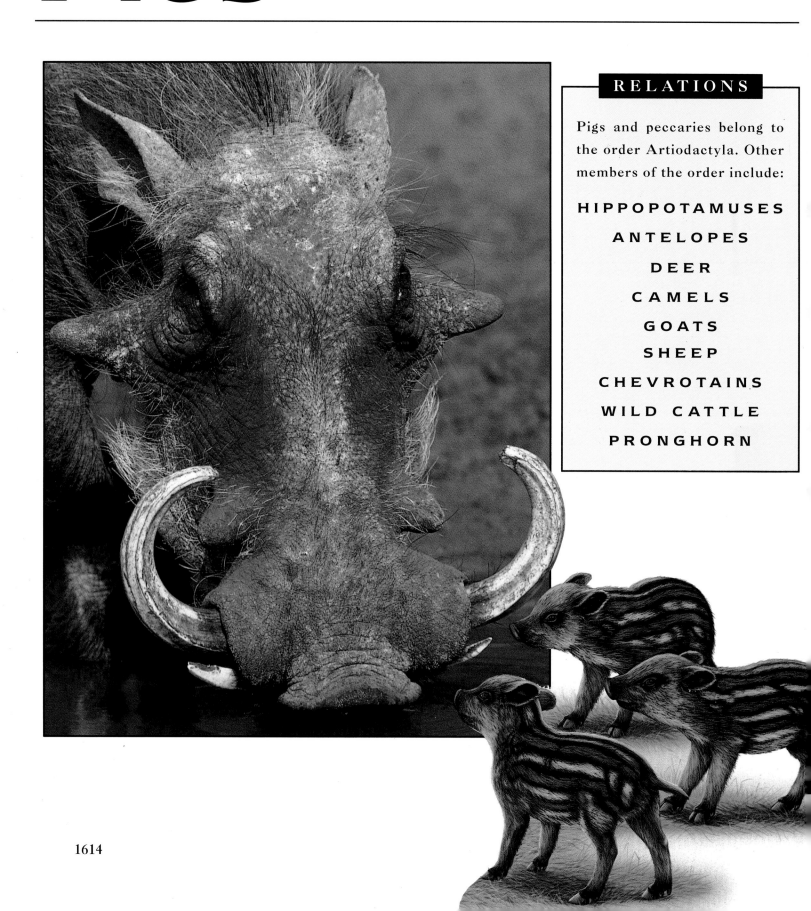

Martin Harvey/The Wildlife Collection

Pigs and peccaries belong to the order of even-toed hoofed mammals, or Artiodactyla, which is divided into three suborders. The pigs, peccaries, and hippopotamuses are the three families that make up the suborder known as the suoids or Suina.

ORDER
Artiodactyla
(even-toed hoofed mammals)

SUBORDER
Suina

PIG FAMILY
Suidae

FIVE GENERA

NINE SPECIES

PECCARY FAMILY
Tayassuidae

TWO GENERA

THREE SPECIES

UGLY BUT SUCCESSFUL

BY NO MEANS THE MOST ATTRACTIVE OF ANIMALS, WILD PIGS AND PECCARIES ARE STRONG, ADAPTABLE, AND INTELLIGENT. THEY ARE COMMONLY FOUND IN MANY PARTS OF THE WORLD

The wild pigs and their relatives the peccaries may not be very attractive, but what they lack in appearance, they make up for in intelligence and adaptability. This has made it possible for them to live in a wide range of different habitats in far-flung places and it has also been at least partly responsible for the successful domestication of wild pigs. Wild pigs are the ancestors of modern farm pigs—animals found in agricultural communities the world over.

Wild pigs have always been of great economic importance to humankind. Since earliest times they have been hunted for their meat and skins and then later, for sport. In medieval Europe the wild boar's strength, aggression, and speed made it one of the favorite beasts of the chase.

The natural distribution of wild pigs stretches across Europe eastward as far as the islands of Southeast Asia and Japan, and south to Africa. This range was later extended by humans, who

introduced the wild boar into North America. In Australasia, the pigs that are found in the wild—known as razorbacks—are feral domestic pigs that have escaped from captivity. Feral pigs also occur in North and South America. Once they have made their homes in the wild, pigs revert to the habits of their ancestors remarkably quickly.

The piglike peccaries are found only in the Americas, from the southern United States to northeastern Argentina. They resemble wild pigs superficially in their general appearance and they have similar habits; they also occupy similar

WILD PIGS HAVE BEEN OF GREAT ECONOMIC IMPORTANCE TO MANKIND SINCE EARLIEST TIMES

habitats and a similar niche in the food chain. However, isolated as they were on the South American continent, the peccaries evolved separately from wild pigs and therefore are sufficiently different to justify being placed in a separate group, or family.

Wild pigs and peccaries are artiodactyls (ar-tee-o-DAK-tils)—hoofed mammals with an even number of toes. Ancestors of wild pigs first appeared as a distinct group in the Eocene (EE-uh-seen) epoch 38 million years ago and were the most primitive of the hoofed mammals. They included paleodonta (pal-ee-o-DONT-a), which had four functional toes

Wild boar piglets are born with striped markings on their coats. These will disappear as they get older, and the scant, stiff, bristly fur will be colored dark gray, black, or brown.

ZEFA

on each foot and cheek teeth with pointed (cusped) surfaces for grinding food. These creatures were succeeded by other piglike mammals, particularly the giant pigs—the entelodonts (en-tel-o-DONTs)—of Europe and North America.

The modern pigs first appeared in the continents of Europe and Asia in the Oligocene (o-LIG-uh-seen) epoch, 37–25 million years ago, and in Africa in the early Miocene (MIE-uh-seen) epoch, 24 million years ago.

Peccaries descended from a group of North American hoofed mammals, among them the platygonus (plat-ee-GO-nus), which lived about 5–2 million years ago Platygonus would have crossed

Rod Williams/Bruce Coleman Ltd.

H. Reinhard/ZEFA

Wild pigs (above) *have been exterminated from much of their former range, including the British Isles. The bizarre-looking babirusa* (top right) *is found on the Southeast Asian islands of Sulawesi, Togian, Sula, and Buru.*

over to South America when the the two continents were joined by a land bridge.

The modern wild pigs and peccaries range in weight from 13–605 lb (6–275 kg). In all species of pig males are larger than females, but in peccaries the sexes are the same size. The body is barrel shaped, the neck short, and the elongated head ends in a movable snout with a disk of cartilage at its tip in which the nostrils are set. The snout contains a number of scent glands and both pigs and peccaries have a highly developed sense of smell as well as excellent hearing.

One of the distinguishing characteristics of pigs and peccaries is their tusks, which are highly specialized canine (eye) teeth. In some species, including the wild boar, only the lower canines have developed into tusks. In others, such as the babirusa, both the upper and lower canines form extraordinarily elaborate tusks.

Tusks are larger in the males of the species than in the females. They are used in battle, as offensive or defensive weapons. Some species, including the three species of peccary, also use them to cut through tough plant materials. Of the remaining teeth, only the wild pigs' back molars are of any importance—used for grinding food. The incisors and premolars usually fall out with age.

Food is usually sought among thick underbrush or dense reed beds, and the animals frequently move with agility through tangled vegetation, impenetrable to most animals. A thick, tough skin protects against injury. In most wild pig species the skin is covered with bristles, although some are almost naked. Others have manes on the head and back and many have skin appendages in the form of warts, humps, or pads on the face. Peccaries are covered in thick, bristly hair with a manelike growth on the neck and they lack facial warts.

All wild pigs have a long tail, either bristled along its length (the wild boar) or with a tassel of bristles at the tip (the warthog). They also have four toes on each foot. As mammals characteristically have five toes, scientists refer to pigs as having lost the first toe, or first digit; the remaining toes being numbered from two to five, not one to four.

The collared and white-lipped peccaries only possess three toes on the hind feet, and the Chacoan peccary, two. All three species have only a hint of a tail. Their stomach is more complex than that of the wild pigs, with three chambers instead of two. The upper tusks are short but sharp, and curve downward, not upward as in the true pigs. The collared and the white-lipped peccaries have more physical features in common with each other than they do with the Chacoan peccary, which more closely resembles the common ancestor, platygonus.

Of the nine species of wild pig, the most widely distributed is the wild boar. It inhabits regions of Europe—where it is now scarce—as well as North Africa and Asia. A creature of woodland and steppe, it can run swiftly and swim well.

Three more species are found only in Africa— the giant forest hog, the warthog, and the bushpig. The giant forest hog ranges across equatorial Africa as far as Liberia and is the largest living species of wild pig. Its upper tusks may measure 8.7 in (220 mm); the lower ones only slightly less. A pair of large, hairless skin protuberances lie below the eyes.

The bushpig and warthog inhabit much of Africa south of the Sahara Desert, and, in the case of the bushpig, Madagascar and Mayotte Island in Comoros. The warthog is distinguishable from all other species by the unique and sturdy upper tusks, which curve outward and upward, the broad snout, and, in the male, the grotesque facial warts. It has a long crest of hair from its head to its rump.

The bushpig is a little larger and heavier than the warthog and its tusks much shorter. It has a white-and-black bristled crest running along the back, and long hairs of the same mixture on the face. These hairs often hide a pair of warts located below the eyes.

The remaining five species of wild pig all inhabit regions of Asia, from Assam, the home of the few remaining pygmy hogs, east to Sulawesi and other Indonesian islands that are inhabited by the Celebes wild pig, the Javan warty pig, the bearded pig, and babirusa. The Celebes, bearded, and Javan warty pigs have well-developed facial warts. The bearded pig is so named because of the long, white hairs on the cheeks. ∎

WARTHOG
Phacochoerus aethiopicus (fack-O-ker-us ath-ee-OP-ih-cus)

The single species is found in Africa, south of the Sahara. It has long upper tusks.

COLLARED PECCARY
Tayassu tajacu (tay-AH-soo taj-A-coo)

So called because of the white ring of hairs around its neck. The white-lipped peccary belongs to the same genus.

PECCARIES

PIGS

Illustrations Alan Male/Linden Artists

CAMELS

HIPPOS

BOVIDS

CHEVROTAIN

EVEN-TOED UNGULATES

GIANT FOREST HOG
Hylochoerus meinertzhageni
(hie-LO-ker-us min-ertz-ha-GEN-ee)

Found in the forest zone from Liberia to southwest Ethiopa and north Tanzania.

THE WILD PIGS' FAMILY TREE

The Suidae family, the wild pigs, contains nine species grouped in five genera and includes the wild boar, the bushpig, the giant forest hog, the warthog, and the babirusa. Peccaries belong to the family Tayassuidae. There are three species: the collared peccary, the white-lipped peccary, and the Chacoan peccary.

WILD BOAR
Sus scrofa (Soos SKRO-fa)

The largest and best-known species in the genus, the wild boar is found in many different habitats. Domestic pigs were developed from these species.

BABIRUSA
Babyrousa babyrussa
(ba-bi-ROO-sa ba-bi-ROO-sa)

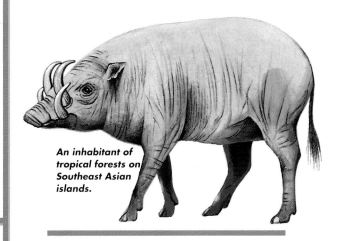

An inhabitant of tropical forests on Southeast Asian islands.

BUSHPIG
Potamochoerus porcus
(pot-ah-MOCK-ah-roos PORE-kus)

MUSK DEER

DEER

GIRAFFE

B/W illustrations Ruth Grewcock

ANATOMY:
WILD BOAR

Smallest of the pigs and peccaries is the pygmy hog. It is 23–26 in (58–66 cm) long and weighs 13–20 lb (6–9 kg). The largest is the giant forest hog, which measures 51–83 in (130–210 cm) and weighs 628–1,333 lb (285–605 kg).

IDENTIFYING BOARS AND SOWS

The boar's head (top) has a long muzzle with well-developed canines. The sow's head (bottom) is much smaller and the teeth are not nearly as powerful as the boar's.

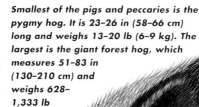

SKIN AND COAT

Very thick skin with coarse bristles. Some individuals grow long hairs on the face, and/or a fairly thick mane of hair. In summer the boar's bristles are rather sparse; in winter they grow closer together.

FEET

Each of the four toes ends in a hoof. The first toe is missing; the third and fourth toes normally bear the animal's full weight. The second and fifth toes have smaller hooves, situated higher up the leg.

Illustrations Wayne Ford/Wildlife Art Agency

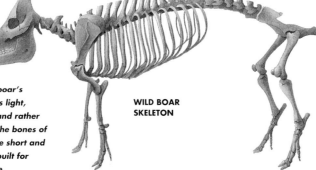

WILD BOAR SKELETON

The wild boar's skeleton is light, delicate, and rather narrow. The bones of the leg are short and thin, but built for endurance.

The foot bones are separate, rather than fused, with the middle two being the longest. The small hooves on the second and fifth toes only touch the ground when the pig walks on marshy or soft ground.

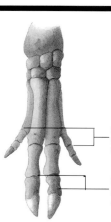

short se
and fift
digits

long thi
and fou
digits

EYES

The warthog's eyes are small but bright. It does not have particularly good vision; smell and hearing are its more developed senses.

SCENT GLANDS AND WARTS

The skin on the nostrils and rump contains scent glands for marking territory and identifying other individuals. Unlike many other wild pigs, the wild boar does not have warts on its face.

LEGS

In spite of its short legs, the wild boar can run fast when necessary. Its normal gait is a trot but it can gallop over short distances when pursued or when in pursuit of prey.

The skull bones are large and bulky. The upper and lower jawbones are elongated and equipped with teeth adapted for grinding food. A long prenasal bone supports the nose.

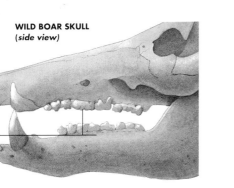

WILD BOAR SKULL
(side view)

grinding teeth

The wild boar has two tusks in the lower jaw—actually the lower canine teeth that have developed into hollow, tubelike structures. They grow out of the side of the jaw, straight up outside the mouth, then curve backward until they point toward the eyes. The curved upper canines fit inside the lower incisors.

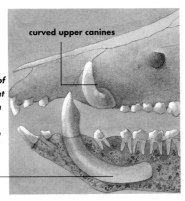

curved upper canines

lower-jaw tusk

COURAGEOUS DEFENDERS

AS THE EVENING DRAWS NEAR, THESE SECRETIVE FORAGERS LEAVE THE SAFETY OF THEIR LEAFY NESTS AND SET OUT ON THEIR NIGHTTIME TRAVELS IN SEARCH OF FOOD

Both pigs and peccaries are generally social animals that live in herds, although in some species of wild pig the older males remain aloof from the others until the breeding season. These mammals congregate wherever there is some form of cover, and they keep very much to themselves. Some wild pig species are active in the late afternoon and at night, particularly in places where they are in danger of being disturbed or molested by people. They spend the day resting in a safe place where they are unlikely to be detected by man or beast. Others, including two of the peccaries, the collared and the Chacoan, hunt during the day. The white-lipped peccary moves about and hunts at periods throughout the day and night.

Peccaries rest in thickets, under large rocks, or in the abandoned burrows of other animals. The wild boar and some other species of wild pig seek protective cover in bushes, reeds, tall grass, dens, between roots of trees, and even in caves. Some

Wild pigs occupy a territory of some 4–4.6 sq miles (10–12 sq km). They mark the limits of this area with secretions from their scent glands, but otherwise they do not seem to be as vigilant at defending their territory as the peccaries. It may be that peccaries are more defensive because they tend to stay in the same place. The collared peccary maintains a territory of 74–690 acres (30–280 ha) and will stoutly defend it against trespassers.

Pigs and peccaries are known to be very courageous in defense of other members of the group and when protecting themselves. This often proves fatal. A wild pig, when cornered or wounded, will fight bravely on, even to the death.

The fighting style of pigs varies according to species. Warthogs (right) *use frontal contact, with the facial warts protecting against the incoming tusks.*

ZEFA

WARTHOGS HAVE IMPRESSIVE-LOOKING UPPER TUSKS BUT IT IS THE SHARPER, SMALLER TUSKS IN THE LOWER JAW THAT INFLICT THE MOST DAMAGE ON ENEMIES

---

construct special shelters out of vegetation. In areas of tall grass they cut the vegetation with their teeth and spread it out to make a grass mat. After crawling underneath the warm blanket they raise their body to lift the now-tangled grass. This is then further entangled with other tall plants, and forms a canopy under which the pigs rest.

The babirusa has an alternative method for constructing a shelter. It bites off large, low-growing leafy branches from trees and bushes and lies underneath them when it rains.

Jonathan Scott/Planet Earth Pictures

Warthogs (above) *often win battles over fierce predators. The lioness has decided enough is enough and the warthog is left in peace.*

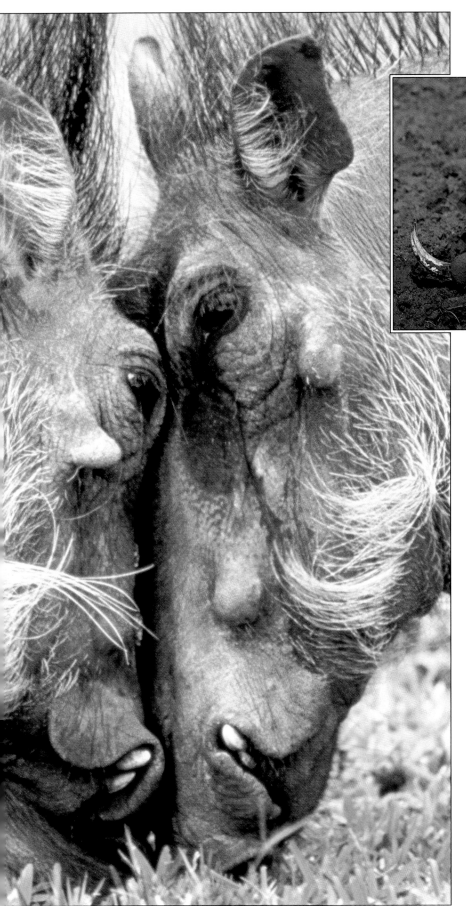

Ian Beames/Ardea

Warthogs love to wallow in mud. It is thought that they do this to help heal minor wounds and to rid themselves of parasites.

Faced by a jaguar or other small cat, a collared peccary may deliberately attract the attention of the predator, thus giving the rest of the herd time to escape. In the Chacoan species, the whole herd may stand close together to protect a wounded or hunted individual. In such situations they may even attempt to charge human hunters.

Many species of wild pig have well-trodden paths throughout their territory connecting the resting places with the feeding areas and the watering holes. Wild pigs like to take frequent, long, and uninterrupted mud baths, so they are usually found

---

PIGS EAT MORE MEAT THAN ANY OTHER HOOFED MAMMAL. THEY ARE VERY FOND OF FROGS AND INSECTS

---

near a source of water. Mud baths get rid of parasites that live on the pigs' bodies, and are necessary for the pigs' general well-being. Wallowing may also cool the body and soothe minor cuts and bruises inflicted in battle or in daily foraging through thickets.

Peccaries are fond of taking sand baths; using their hooves, they paw at the sand, throwing it up against their bodies. Such activity presumably serves the same cleansing function as the pigs' mud baths. Both types of mammal are clean in their habits, and in no way deserve the image of the "dirty" creatures of folklore.

Wild pigs also regularly visit certain places where they can rub their bodies against trees, rocks, and other structures. They will also frequent natural salt licks and those put out for cattle and deer. ∎

HABITATS

Joe van Os/The Image Bank

The warthog is an inhabitant of the African savanna grasslands and woodlands. It usually forages and drinks in small groups. It eats mainly grass and plucks the tips of the grass off with its lips. It is active during the day.

The wild pigs occupy a wide variety of habitats across Europe, Asia, and Africa north and south of the Sahara Desert. In Europe they are found mainly in broad-leaved woodlands dominated by oak trees and in Asia in tropical forests and mangroves. Forest and savanna grasslands are the preferred habitats of most African species, although the giant forest hog also frequents the transitional zone between forest and grassland. In East and central Africa giant hogs are found in small numbers in the highlands and montane (mountain) forests.

The thorn forest of the Chaco in South America covers a total of some 243,000 sq miles (630,000 sq km). The driest part of the Chaco is in the west and is home to the Chacoan peccary. Here, the mean annual temperature exceeds 75°F (24°C), with rainfall of between 8 in (200 mm) a year in the

Survival Anglia

The three species of peccary live in Central and South America. Their habitats range from dry and wet forest regions to woody grasslands and dense thickets. They are found at various altitudes. They are active during the day when they feed on roots, seeds, and fruits.

DISTRIBUTION

KEY

- ■ WILD BOAR
- ▨ WARTHOG
- ■ COLLARED PECCARY
- ■ BABIRUSA
- ■ GIANT FOREST HOG
- ▨ BUSHPIG

The wild boar lives in Europe, North Africa, Asia (including the southeast islands of Indonesia), Japan, and Taiwan. Feral populations are found in North and South America and Australasia.

The giant forest hog makes its home in east, west, and central regions of Africa. Also found in Africa, south of the Sahara, are the warthog and the bushpig, the latter also being found on the island of Madagascar.

The babirusa is confined to the Indonesian islands of Sulawesi, Togian, Sula, and Buru.

Peccaries are found from the southwestern United States to northern Argentina.

KEY FACTS

- ● As a family the wild pigs have no special adaptations that restrict them to a particular habitat. This has been a major factor in their widespread distribution.

- ● Apart from their need to be near water, the major limitation on the spread of wild pigs is probably deep, snow-covered areas, which prohibit them from searching for food.

- ● The straight tail of the wild boar is used for swatting flying insects or twitched when it is cross. It uses its snout to root for food.

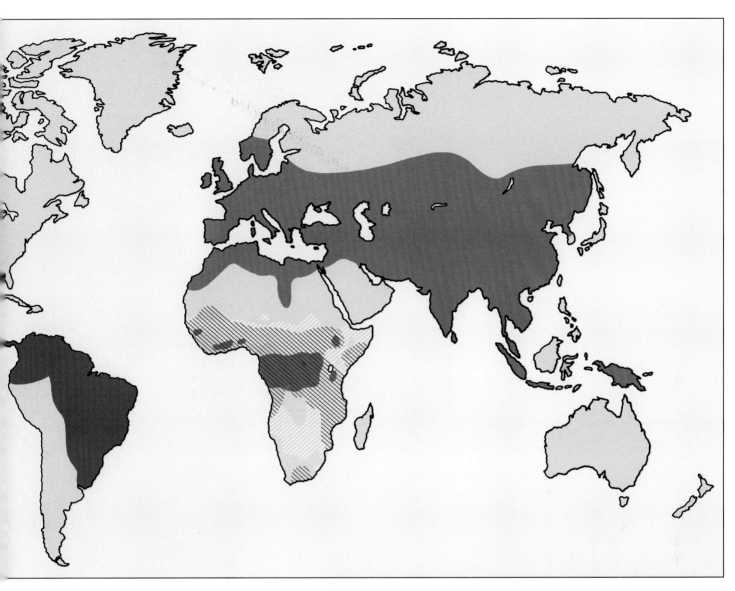

western parts to 35.5 in (900 mm) in the east. The dry season lasts for five months.

Vegetation in the thorn forests consists largely of emergent trees and a dense underlayer of brush consisting mainly of acacia. Bromeliads and cacti grow on the ground. Cacti are the main food of the Chacoan peccary, but it also feeds on acacia fruit, bromeliads, and low-growing herbs from which it gets most of the moisture it needs. In the wetter, more easterly regions the vegetation of the dry areas is replaced with grassland dotted with palms.

Jaguar, puma, and ocelot occur in the Chaco and often prey on the peccary, which forages in small herds of up to ten animals. The peccary is very brave when confronting the enemy and is at its most vulnerable when it strays from the herd.

The bushpig, or red river hog, is found in Africa south of the Sahara and also in Madagascar. It inhabits both grasslands and woodlands.

Nigel Dennis/NHPA

Tropical forest species include the white-lipped and collared peccaries of South and Central America, although some also occur in oak grasslands and on the chaparral (thorny scrub, originally of evergreen oaks). The babirusa, bearded pig, and Celebes wild pig inhabit similar forests in Asia while the giant forest hog and bushpig are sometimes found in the forests in Africa.

In tropical forests everywhere the sunlight is strong and the mean monthly temperature is greater than 68°F (20°C). Almost constant sun combined with varying amounts of rain determine the type of vegetation in tropical forests. Where rainfall is moderate—often less than 20 in (50 cm) a year—trees are limited in type and density. Acacia, or thorn trees, are typical. These trees are deciduous, losing their leaves in the dry season in order to conserve water. Animal life is limited to those creatures that can survive on smaller animals or dried vegetation and need little or no water.

In those areas where rainfall is more abundant, but occurs mainly at definite periods in the year, the vegetation is more luxuriant. This is the monsoon forest, characteristic of parts of southern India, the

FOCUS ON

THE BLACK FOREST

A mountainous area in southwest Germany, this region is one of the last refuges in western Europe of the wild boar. This area encompasses 2,320 sq miles (6,009 sq km); its highest peak is Feldberg, which lies at 4,897 ft (1,493 m) above sea level. The region is divided in two by the deep Kinzig Valley. On the lower slopes are some of the remnants of the broad-leaved forest that once covered much of Germany, the typical temperate woods of oak and beech. Here the climate is moderate with a plentiful rainfall and the seasons are well marked. Summers are warm and winters cold.

The animals that inhabit the woods cope with cold winter conditions in different ways. They either hibernate, living on food stored in the body during the summer, migrate to warmer countries farther south, or adapt to living in a harsh environment where food in winter is scarce.

The wild boar is one of the latter, surviving because it has an extremely varied diet and a coat that becomes thicker as winter approaches.

BLACK FOREST CLIMATE

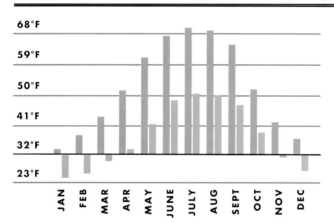

| MAXIMUM AVERAGE TEMPERATURE |
| MINIMUM AVERAGE TEMPERATURE |

The Black Forest is carpeted in snow during the winter months. At the higher altitudes alpine plants abound in spring but the forest really comes to life in the summer and supports vineyards, rich pastures for cattle, and a profusion of wildflowers.

foothills of the Himalayas, and mainland Southeast Asia. Trees are deciduous but more varied. In the Indian monsoon forest the trees are bare of leaves in summer and in leaf in winter.

With the arrival of the monsoon the water holes, or jheels, fill to overflowing. Many of these depressions are fairly large and form small lakes. In the dry season they shrink to small pools fringed with muddy beaches. In both dry and wet seasons the jheels are the favored haunts of wild boars, providing them with water and the much-needed mud for wallowing. The wild boars are joined at these watering places by exotic birds such as the lesser whistling teal, demoiselle crane, purple heron, and painted storks. ∎

NEIGHBORS

The mixed woodlands of the Black Forest attract a host of animals and birds. Rare butterflies flutter across the gentle grass slopes found at lower altitudes and there are many wildflowers.

RED DEER

Essentially a woodland animal, the red deer is common in the forest, living in protected sites.

EUROPEAN HEDGEHOG

Ideal habitat for the hedgehog, which can be seen shuffling on its nighttime hunting forays.

Neighbor illustrations Ruth Grewcock

THE BLACK FOREST

The Black Forest is bordered by France to the east and Switzerland to the south and shares features with both. The Rhine River also partially borders it. The area takes its name from the many dark, tree-covered summits, a mixture of coniferous trees and broad-leaved woodland.

RHINOCEROS BEETLE

So called because of the "horn" on its head, the beetle uses the horn to lift and carry rival males away.

WILDCAT

Resembling the domestic tabby, the wildcat is heavier. It is confined to wooded and inaccessible mountainsides.

CAPERCAILLIE

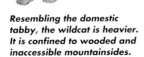

The capercaillie is the largest member of the grouse family. It eats the buds and shoots of pines.

EUROPEAN BADGER

A typical woodland animal, the nocturnal badger lives in the higher regions of the Black Forest.

WOOD ANT

Close to the bottom of the food chain, wood ants are preyed upon by great spotted woodpeckers.

FOOD AND FEEDING

Wild pigs and peccaries are omnivorous; they eat a wide variety of plant and animal food, including carrion. The wild boar's diet is typical: fungi, leaves, roots, acorns and beechmast, bulbs, tubers, and fruit, plus earthworms, snails, birds' eggs, and small reptiles and mammals. Boars and other wild pigs that live on or near the fringes of forest near cultivated land frequently make a nuisance of themselves by feeding on crops. They frequently spoil much more than they eat and therefore incur the wrath of the farmer.

On grasslands and in open woodland the warthog feeds on grass, roots, berries, and the bark of young trees. They also feed on carrion when necessary. During a prolonged dry season in Nairobi in 1961 warthogs were observed feeding on

> MOST WILD PIGS USE THE SNOUT FOR FORAGING ON THE GROUND AND IN SO DOING TURN OVER A LARGE QUANTITY OF SOIL

the carcass of a wildebeest that had either starved to death or died of thirst.

When it is feeding the warthog shuffles along uttering many grunts. Its eyes are set farther back on its head than those of other pigs, positioned just in front of its ears. This enables it to look farther

HOW WARTHOGS EAT

Because of its short neck the warthog has to kneel down to eat. To protect the wrists from damage on the hard ground, the joints are covered in wide calluses.

Illustrations William Oliver/Wildlife Art Agency

ALONGSIDE MAN

PIGGY TRUFFLES

The domesticated pig has retained the wild boar's highly developed sense of smell. Humans make use of this in locating that most prized of all edible fungi, the truffle, which for centuries has been regarded as one of the most exquisite delicacies.

Truffles flourish in open woodland on alkaline (limey) soils, usually among the roots of trees at depths of up to 12 in (30 cm). Gourmets regard French truffles as being among the finest, particularly those that grow in the truffle grounds (*truffières*) in Périgord and the Vaucluse department of France. Truffle-hunting pigs are kept on a leash and are muzzled: They are as appreciative of the flavor of truffles as their human handlers.

Telegraph Colour Library

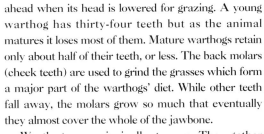

ahead when its head is lowered for grazing. A young warthog has thirty-four teeth but as the animal matures it loses most of them. Mature warthogs retain only about half of their teeth, or less. The back molars (cheek teeth) are used to grind the grasses which form a major part of the warthogs' diet. While other teeth fall away, the molars grow so much that eventually they almost cover the whole of the jawbone.

Warthogs are principally grazers. They gather succulent grasses and grass seeds with their lips, or pluck them up with their upper incisors. During the dry season when grass is scarce they use the upper part of the snout, the rhinatrum, to dig rhizomes (underground stems) from the baked earth.

The babirusa does not root with its snout unless foraging in muddy or swampy ground. It is typically omnivorous, eating a wide range of foods including small mammals. The babirusa has strong jaws and teeth, and is said to be able to crack the hard shells of nuts with its jaws.

Where food is abundant wild pigs remain in their chosen location, but should food become scarce they migrate to new feeding grounds. Wild boars, for example, may travel some considerable distance to find an area that will satisfy their feeding requirements, and have even been known to turn up in places where they have never previously appeared. The bearded pigs of Borneo's rain forests feed on fallen fruit that becomes locally abundant at different times of the year. To insure that they have a constant supply the pigs establish migratory routes between feeding areas and travel from one to another as a new crop ripens. They sometimes swim across wide rivers on their journeys.

Although peccaries are omnivorous they prefer fruit, seeds, and plant roots. The collared peccary, like the Chacoan, also feeds on cacti. Peccaries have a three-chambered stomach, which is more complex than the simple two-chambered stomach of the wild pigs. It is thought that their stomach contains beneficial microorganisms that aid digestion. ■

A PECCARY EATING CACTUS

The collared peccaries have strong jaws, which enable them to cut through tough roots and plants. Wild pigs chew in a semicircular fashion.

WILD BOAR AT WATER

This species does not stray far from water. It drinks frequently and also searches for frogs around the edges of pools.

SOCIAL STRUCTURE

The basic unit of wild pigs is a nursery consisting of a female and her litter. When the young are three to four months old she joins up with a number of other females and their young, forming a herd, or sounder. The sounder is matriarchal in structure and is dominated by one of the older sows. Herds of wild boars may come together in the autumn to form bands of up to fifty females with young. There may also be separate, smaller herds of immature bachelor males. Older, sexually active males tend to lead a solitary life. Most of them join the female

THE WILD BOAR USES A VARIETY OF SOUNDS FROM SQUEAKS TO GRUNTS TO COMMUNICATE WITH OTHERS

herds at the beginning of the rutting season and leave again immediately after mating.

Where wild pigs are numerous, large herds sometimes break up, with small groups of mothers and daughters moving away but remaining in the vicinity near the primary group. These related clans share the same feeding grounds, nesting sites, and watering holes.

The form of social organization described above is typical of the wild boar, among others. In the bushpig, the herd, or drove, is dominated by a boss boar, its function being to keep the herd

under control. In the boss boar's absence a younger male, the deputy, takes over. The boars are massive and ferocious and bravely defend the herd against predators.

In India the tiny pygmy hog lives in small herds of between five and six, with occasionally as many as fifteen to twenty. Some observers have reported that male pygmy hogs typically live apart from the herds, but do not separate themselves entirely. They remain near at hand and, like the bushpig, are ready to defend the herd as necessary. Other observers report that, in some cases, the male remains with the group all year around.

Peccaries live in mixed groups of males, females, and young. There is no leader, although when a herd is on the move they tend to follow the one that is out in front, frequently a female. The herds of collared peccaries usually number between 5 and 15 individuals, those of the white-lipped up to 100 and the Chacoan peccary 2 to 10. Within the herd there are smaller units of family groups. These 3 species exhibit what is known as "smell-sharing" behavior. They engage in mutual grooming, at the same time marking each other with scent from a gland below the eyes. This appears to be a coordinating factor when the herd moves off together, and also reinforces the group as a social unit.

STRIPED PIGLETS

The wild boar produces up to a dozen piglets in a litter. The piglets have a coat of stripes that helps to camouflage them in the grass. The piglets stay striped for about six months, and it is another six months before they acquire the color of their parents.

AMAZING FACTS

BABIRUSA'S TUSKS

Pat Morris

The tusks of the Indonesian babirusa are more spectacular than those of any other wild pig. While in most species the tusks grow from the sides of the jaw, in the babirusa the upper tusks grow directly through the muzzle and curve back toward the eyes. In some individuals they will grow so much that the tips reenter the skin.

Although extremely impressive these tusks are not the babirusa's main line of offense. This function is fulfilled by the lower tusks, which are daggerlike and much more dangerous.

Social grooming plays an important part in wild pig communities. These animals like close physical contact and when resting will get as close to one another as possible. Grooming includes massaging with the tip of the snout and running the teeth or lips through the other pig's hair and mane.

At times, the bearded pigs of Borneo associate with other species that are helpful to them, particularly flocks of crowned wood pigeons. These birds benefit the pigs by picking ticks from the pigs' skin, and at the first sign of danger the birds will give the alarm. The birds benefit from this relationship because the pigs allow them to take worms and other invertebrates from the soil where the pigs are also feeding.

VOCAL COMMUNICATION
Wild pigs and peccaries communicate largely by sound. Warthogs and wild boars utter grunts and squeaks and have special calls for maintaining contact with members of the group, giving warnings and threats,

MARKING TERRITORY
Although wild boars are not territorial, home ranges are marked with lip-gland pheromones. Salivary foam is also produced. The wild boars rub their mouths around trees and other structures within the range. Each home range measures about 3.9–7.7 sq miles (10–20 sq km).

Illustrations Steve Kingston

Clem Haagner/Ardea

A female warthog gives birth to up to four young. She leaves them for most of the day, returning at noon and in the evening to feed them. They start to leave the den after about a week.

example, wild boars fight shoulder to shoulder, slashing out at their opponent's side with their tusks as they bring their heads up from below. They are, however, at least partly protected by a shield of thickened skin covered with matted hair. This develops on both sides of the body just prior to the rutting season, and covers an area from the shoulders to the last rib. As the animal moves, the shield slides backward and forward, and does not stretch like the skin on other parts of the body.

When fighting, giant forest hogs come together head to head, making contact with the forehead. The force with which they meet could cause severe damage to the skull and brain, but they are afforded some protection by thickening of the skull in the area of the forehead.

NESTS AND DENS

Pigs are somewhat unique among the ungulates in constructing nests or occupying dens and similar protected spaces in which to

DOMINANT MALE BUSHPIG

Living in family groups, each family is led by a dominant boar who will also protect the family. Should juvenile males try to intrude on the adult male's feeding place, he will chase them off.

Illustrations Steve Kingston

and signaling submission.

The sounds made by peccaries are equally diverse. The collared peccary makes a laughlike cry when engaged in aggressive behavior and a call similar to a cough when calling members of the group together. Infants in distress make a shrill clicking noise and adults raise the alarm with a "woof" repeated many times. An angry or annoyed peccary chatters its teeth, which produces a rasping noise. While eating, collared peccaries make an odd, clear nasal sound.

Competition for food can sometimes lead to minor skirmishes between individuals of a herd, when one pig will attempt to shove another away. Serious conflict between adult sexually active males occurs during the rutting season when they fight for the right to mate with the females. The wounds inflicted during these battles can be serious.

Various species of wild pig have specialized battle techniques, and have developed equally specialized defenses to help protect them from their opponents. For

rest, although some, such as the babirusa, do neither. Instead, they make do with a shallow depression in the ground. The wild boars make shallow beds, which in cold weather they plump out with more plant material. At the opposite extreme, the warthog utilizes hollows under rocks, natural holes, or those of a suitable size that have been deserted by other animals, such as the aardvark. The aardvark and the warthog are so alike in size that in most cases the warthog does not have to enlarge the tunnels of its burrow. Warthogs have a habit of backing into their den in order to keep an eye out for any predator that might be in the vicinity. It is usually only the young that enter headfirst, and in these instances an adult will always be the last to enter—backward. ■

FACIAL WARTS

Facial warts are a typical feature of the wild pigs. They are particularly noticeable in the warthog and are also present in the bushpig and Javan warty pig. The main function of the warts is to protect the animal from blows inflicted by an opponent's curving tusks. This is particularly so in the case of the bushpig, which engages head to head in battles. Each male crosses its snout over that of its opponent and, in doing so, attacks the face with its tusks.

HEAD TO HEAD
Each species of pig has its own method of fighting. In the warthog (above) contact is frontal. The bushpig (bottom) crosses snouts. Both species are protected by warts.

LIFE CYCLE

The courtship and mating cycle of wild boars has been more thoroughly studied than other species, but most wild pigs follow a similar pattern. Adult male boars that have led a solitary life during the past year join the sounders of receptive females at the beginning of the rutting season, which in temperate climates occurs once a year and in tropical climates may occur at any time. The boars may have to travel long distances in order to reach the herd, often arriving exhausted and hungry. Where there are young boars present that have not yet left the mother the older male's first act will be to send them off.

Both wild boars and warthogs will persistently follow a female and drive her around in circles, all the time uttering a strange noise, which has been described as sounding like a "clattering motor." At the same time, the male will repeatedly nudge the female, massage her roughly with his snout, and attempt to rest his snout on her rump. The latter action has the result of making the female stand still. Mating occurs several times, and at the end of the rutting season the male leaves the herd to pursue his solitary life again.

in SIGHT

A WARTHOG'S DEN

The female warthog gives birth in a den (perhaps an abandoned aardvark's nest) that she has lined with leaves and other plant material. She may also use stems and branches to construct a rough canopy over the nest. In cold weather, the piglets benefit from this extra protection because they have only a small amount of hair at birth.

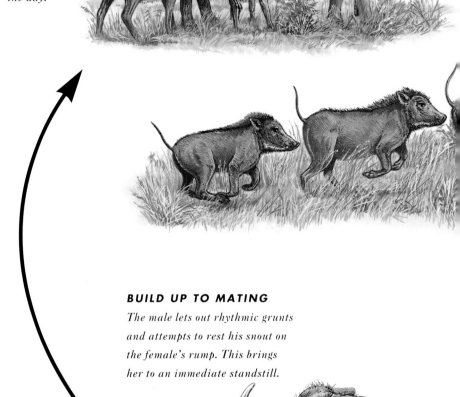

SUCKLING

The warthog sow has four teats, but the piglets have solid food after one week. The mother leaves her young for long periods during the day.

BUILD UP TO MATING

The male lets out rhythmic grunts and attempts to rest his snout on the female's rump. This brings her to an immediate standstill.

GROWING UP

The life of a young warthog

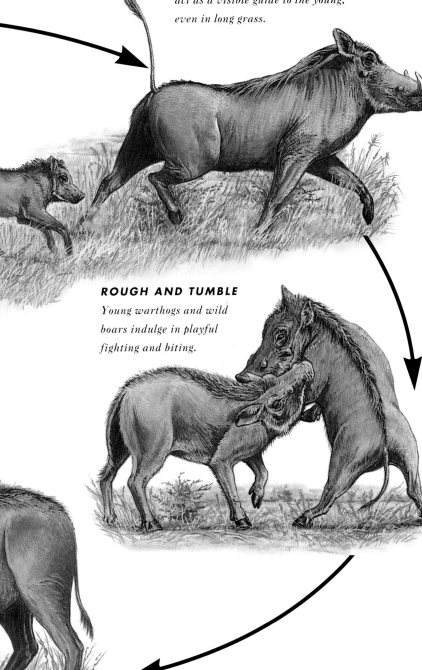

FOLLOW ME

Adult warthogs always run with their tails held vertical so that they act as a visible guide to the young, even in long grass.

ROUGH AND TUMBLE

Young warthogs and wild boars indulge in playful fighting and biting.

Illustrations Toni Hargreaves

FROM BIRTH TO DEATH

WILD BOAR

GESTATION: 170–175 DAYS

LITTER SIZE: FIRST LITTER, 3–4; SUCCEEDING ONES UP TO 12

BREEDING SEASON: SEASONAL IN TEMPERATE ZONES, NONSEASONAL IN TROPICS

MAMMAE: 6 PAIRS

EYES OPEN: AT BIRTH

FIRST SOLID FOOD: 14 DAYS

WEANING: 12 WEEKS

INDEPENDENCE: 2 YEARS

SEXUAL MATURITY: 18–24 MONTHS

FULL ADULT SIZE: 5–6 YEARS

LONGEVITY: 15–20 YEARS

WARTHOG

GESTATION: 170–175 DAYS

LITTER SIZE: 1–8, USUALLY 2–4

BREEDING SEASON: SEASONAL

MAMMAE: 2 PAIRS

EYES OPEN: AT BIRTH

FIRST SOLID FOOD: 7 DAYS

WEANING: 21 WEEKS

INDEPENDENCE: 12 MONTHS

SEXUAL MATURITY: 12–20 MONTHS

FULL ADULT SIZE: 5–6 YEARS

LONGEVITY: 12–15 YEARS

The female remains in the herd until she is ready to farrow (give birth). She then leaves and finds a suitable place to make a nest—somewhere quiet that is hidden by dense plant cover.

The piglets are small and rounded in shape. Wild boar piglets have a striped coat, warthog piglets are grayish pink and not striped. The piglets begin to crawl about as soon as they are born and scramble to suck at the teat. The female wild boar has twelve teats and the warthog four. If more piglets are born than there are teats, all may still survive if the female is well fed.

Both wild boar and warthog piglets remain in the nest for some time. The wild boar sow stays with her young most of the time and only leaves for short periods. When she does so, she will often cover the piglets with nesting material. The warthog sow leaves her young for long periods during the day, returning at intervals to suckle them and returning at nightfall. After a week the piglets leave the nest

MANY WILD BOARS DIE BEFORE THE AGE OF TWELVE MONTHS. THE CAUSES INCLUDE DISEASE, COLD, AND PREDATORS

and begin to follow the sow, but for some time they continue to return to the nest at night. Although they begin to eat some solid foods within the first few weeks of life, the piglets continue to suckle for about three months. Once the piglets have been weaned, the sow returns with them to the herd.

The young males leave their mother when they are about twelve months old, or before the sow has her next litter. However, females may stay with the mother until they are eighteen months old. Although males are sexually mature by two years they are not usually able to compete successfully for the females until they are five years old. ∎

SAVING THEIR BACON

A COMBINATION OF FOREST CLEARANCE, DISEASE, AND HUNTING IS PUTTING WILD PIGS AT RISK, AND UNLESS CONSERVATION MEASURES ARE QUICKLY IMPLEMENTED, MANY OF THE RARER SPECIES WILL DIE OUT

Martin Harvey/Wildlife Collection

The pygmy hog is one of the world's rarest mammals (inset). The warthog (main picture) is also under threat because of habitat destruction.

The widespread transformation of the European landscape from forest and wood to cultivated land took place many centuries ago. This deforestation was in large part responsible for the decline in populations of many large forest mammals—the wild boar among them—although hunting for meat, hides, and sport were also contributing factors.

Some of these mammals, such as the lynx, brown bear, and wolf, have probably disappeared from Europe forever, and the bison exists only in captivity. The fate of the wild boar was better, for the animal survives today in Europe in isolated patches. It is found in the remnants of the great forests, from parts of Scandinavia south to the Mediterranean. In Asia it is present in much larger numbers and over a much wider area, and overall the populations of wild boar are said to be satisfactory. This applies equally to the wild pigs of Africa. Of the other species restricted to Asia and Central and South America, the pygmy hog

> THE BABIRUSA'S STOMACH HAS AN EXTRA SAC, WHICH POSSIBLY HELPS IT TO DIGEST CELLULOSE

is critically endangered and the babirusa, Javan warty pig, and the collared peccary are vulnerable. The Chacoan peccary is classified as endangered.

THE WAY TO EXTINCTION

Destruction of habitats on a worldwide scale is one of the main contributing factors to the decline and, in some cases, the extinction of many species of plants and animals. This is no less true for the wild pigs and peccaries, which are under pressure particularly from forest clearance and the overmanagement of grasslands. They are often the victims of economic and/or political policies and programs involving the felling of timber for profit, the creation of agricultural

land, or the establishment of human communities and recreation facilities. On grassland that is managed by regular burning to stimulate and renew plant growth, pigs are not only in immediate danger of injury and death, they also suffer from a depletion of their food supply because the former rich diversity of food is replaced by fewer and specialized fire-resistant plants.

Wild pigs that inhabit grasslands and steppe are often in direct competition for food with domestic livestock or other species. Where food is scarce this can have long-lasting consequences. The Javan warty pig, with a population already in decline, is an example of a species that is threatened by the need to compete for food with the wild boar, a species that is not only more numerous but also has the same dietary needs. This may occur in areas where food is already scarce because of habitat loss.

Joe Blossom/NHPA

THEN & NOW

The map below shows the ranges of the giant forest hog and the pygmy hog, which is now found only in a small area of northwest Assam.

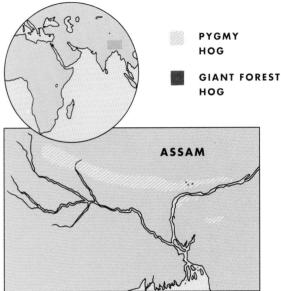

PYGMY HOG

GIANT FOREST HOG

ASSAM

The pygmy hog originally occurred south of the Himalayan foothills from northeast Uttar Pradesh through southern Nepal and northwest Bengal to northwest Assam. Today it is known only in very few places in northwest Assam, most notably in the Manas Wildlife Sanctuary and the Barnadi Wildlife Sanctuary. Numbers have been estimated at fifty individuals in the Barnadi sanctuary and not more than twice that number in the Manas sanctuary; the exact populations are unknown. The giant forest hog is one of the symptomless carriers of African swine fever and has been a victim of eradication campaigns.

The presence of domestic livestock in areas inhabited by wild pigs and peccaries not only puts a strain on food resources but can result in the spread of disease in both wild and domestic stock. One of the contributing factors to the population decline of the Chacoan peccary is the death of many individuals from an as-yet-unknown disease. There is a strong possibility that they may be the victims of foot-and-mouth disease or bovine rabies as a result of the relatively recent introductions (1970s) of domestic animals into the area.

In Africa, sleeping sickness in humans and livestock is indirectly but unarguably linked to warthogs and bushpigs. Both the disease known as the East African type, which occurs in humans, and the similar disease in livestock known as ngana, are spread by animal microbes called trypanosomes, which are carried by the bloodsucking savanna tsetse fly, which is particularly partial to the blood of these wild pigs, humans, and livestock. The wild pigs therefore facilitate the spread of the disease.

Warthogs, giant forest hogs, and bushpigs are also responsible for the spread of African swine fever (ASF). This disease is carried by the tampan, a soft-bodied tick, and is lethal to domestic swine but does not affect wild pigs, which only carry the disease.

Efforts made to control or eradicate these diseases have included programs to exterminate the bushpig, warthog, and giant forest hog in those areas where domestic stock is threatened. In some areas the programs appear to have been successful in controlling the disease.

HUNTING

The hunting of peccaries and wild pigs occurs most noticeably among the people of South America, who kill the white-lipped and collared peccaries for their skins, and among the inhabitants of northern Sulawesi, who trade in the babirusa's meat. The hides of the Chacoan peccary are not as highly valued as those of the other two species and therefore hunting pressure on them is not as great, even though they are hunted for their meat.

The efforts of government conservation organizations and other interested parties to reverse or contain population losses have included the establishment of national parks, wildlife sanctuaries, and captive-breeding programs, as well as giving the species legal protection. The Chacoan peccary is legally protected against commercial exploitation in Argentina, and in Paraguay it is included in the

PIGS AND PECCARIES IN DANGER

THE CHART BELOW SHOWS HOW THE INTERNATIONAL UNION FOR THE CONSERVATION OF NATURE (IUCN), OR THE WORLD CONSERVATION UNION CLASSIFIES THE STATUS OF SOME SPECIES OF PIGS AND PECCARIES:

BABIRUSA	VULNERABLE
VISAYAN WARTY PIG	VULNERABLE
WESTERN BEARDED PIG	VULNERABLE
PYGMY HOG	VULNERABLE
RYUKYU ISLAND'S WILD PIG	VULNERABLE
JAVAN AND BAWEAN WARTY PIGS	VULNERABLE

VULNERABLE INDICATES THAT THE ANIMAL IS LIKELY TO MOVE INTO THE ENDANGERED CATEGORY IF THINGS CONTINUE AS THEY ARE.

The collared peccary is being studied in the southwestern United States, its northernmost range.

official protection of all wildlife species. The babirusa was given full legal protection by the Indonesian government in 1981. Both species are, in some areas, contained in a few wildlife preserves.

The pygmy hog is confined to two wildlife sanctuaries, one of which, the Manas sanctuary, was among the first to be designated a tiger preserve, an event that occurred in 1973. This sanctuary was also distinguished in 1966 when it was declared a World Heritage Site by UNESCO (United Nations Educational, Scientific and Cultural Organization). This sanctuary was also the first to be designated a tiger preserve.

All three of these endangered and threatened species (the babirusa, Chacoan peccary, and pygmy hog) have been the subject of captive breeding at one time or another. Attempts to breed the pygmy hog have as yet not yielded any results, but the breeding of the babirusa in zoological parks has been relatively successful. At the end of 1989, a total of 131 individuals had been born in zoos in Europe, Indonesia, and the United States. In a special project set up in the Paraguayan Chaco in 1986, twenty-nine Chacoan peccaries had been born at a captive breeding station by 1992. ∎

Des & Jen Bartlett/Survival Anglia

INTO THE FUTURE

According to the International Union for the Conservtion of Nature (IUCN), the pygmy hog is among the most endangered of all mammals and has the highest priority rating of all pigs. In 1984, it was included in the first IUCN/WWF listing of the twelve most threatened animal species.

In the opinion of the IUCN, the small population in the Manas Wildlife Sanctuary offers the best possibility for ensuring the continuation of the species, but immediate action is necessary if there is to be any success. The organization makes a number of recommendations for action, including the following:

• The problems confronting the authorities in the Manas Wildlife Sanctuary—political agitation and illegal immigration—must be resolved so that the sanctuary can be brought under control by the appropriate authorities and the remaining recommendations can be implemented.

PREDICTION

MORE RESEARCH

Hopefully, field studies assessing the population size and distribution of the babirusa will lead to a better understanding of its needs. And as captive-breeding programs become more effective, some vulnerable species, such as the babirusa, will be reintroduced into suitable habitats.

• Adequate protection must be ensured for all wildlife in the sanctuary, and further field studies must be undertaken in order to assess the size of the population, its distribution, and the location, size, and number of any other populations of pygmy hog.

• Effective captive-breeding programs must be started so that possible reintroductions can take place.

For the Javan warty pig the solution appears to be to relocate as many of the present population as possible to suitable habitats where they will not have to compete so hard with the wild boars. ∎

ACTION—NOW

In spite of some successes in captive breeding in the past few years, the efforts made to date have sadly had little or no effect on declining populations of wild pig species. This may be because laws prohibiting hunting, for example, are unenforced or unenforceable, or because authorities have been unable to put plans into action, often for political reasons. In northwest Assam, civil unrest and illegal immigration have delayed the implementation of proposals to save the pygmy hog. In the Chaco there are not enough preserves, and too few animals have been made available for captive breeding.

Unless problems such as these can be overcome, the vulnerable and endangered species of pig and peccary will be added to the list of extinct species in the very near future.

THE OUTLOOK

The outlook for the Chacoan peccary depends on how successful the IUCN's recommendations are—and if they are carried out in time. Among other matters, the organization reports that private preserves should be established in areas where significant numbers of peccaries survive. It also reports that the possibility of relocating some peccaries into national parks should be investigated, and that local awareness of conservation problems should be increased through education.

Although captive breeding of the babirusa has been relatively successful compared to other vulnerable species, the animals at present in captivity would benefit from the introduction of other individuals from the wild in order to prevent inbreeding.

PLATYPUSES

RELATIONS

The platypus and echidnas are members of the order Monotremata. There are two families and three species as shown:

PLATYPUS

LONG-BEAKED ECHIDNA

SHORT-BEAKED ECHIDNA

Tom McHugh/Oxford Scientific Films

EGG-LAYING MAMMALS

THE DUCKBILLED PLATYPUS AND ECHIDNAS ARE AMONG THE OLDEST AND POSSIBLY THE STRANGEST-LOOKING MAMMALS. THEY ARE FOUND ONLY IN AUSTRALASIA AND ARE THE ONLY MAMMALS TO LAY EGGS

Echidnas and the platypus, collectively known as monotremes, belong to a small order of animals called Monotremata, of which they are the only surviving members. Along with the marsupials, they are the most primitive of all the mammals.

Together, the monotremes and marsupials are distinguished from all other placental mammals by their method of reproduction. In particular, the monotremes are unique in that they lay eggs, and although their females have mammary glands, they do not have nipples. On the other hand, marsupials give birth to tiny, near-embryonic young. Both of these are unlike the placental majority of mammals that carry their young within the uterus (womb) until they are well developed.

Two families make up the order of Monotremata. These have a total of just three surviving species, all of which are confined to Australasia. There are the single species of the duckbill, or platypus, family and the two species of the echidna, or spiny anteater, family. Despite laying eggs and sharing certain anatomical similarities with reptiles, the monotremes exhibit the two essential mammalian features—body hair and mammary glands. Male monotremes have a horny spur on each hind ankle, which in the platypus can deliver poison from a gland located beneath the skin on the upper surface of the femur (the thigh bone).

Many references are made to the strange combination of mammalian and reptilian characteristics that are exhibited by the monotremes. In summary, they are mammalian regarding their brains, hair, warm blood, hearts, larynxes, and diaphragms,

> WHEN ON LAND, THE PLATYPUS IS
> ABLE TO ROLL UP THE WEBBING
> ON ITS FEET SO IT CAN THEN USE
> ITS CLAWS TO AID WALKING

but in their skeletons and egg-laying habits they resemble reptiles. They are interesting because they suggest an intermediate stage between these two animal classes. There are certainly many things still to be discovered from these extraordinary creatures, whose general structure perhaps has remained almost unchanged for about 200 million years, from Triassic or Jurassic times.

THE ECHIDNAS

The two species of echidnas are each covered with coarse hair and their backs also carry spines. They have elongated, slender snouts, lack teeth, and have very weak jaws. Their strong limbs

The platypus spends most of its time in the water.
It builds its burrows in riverbanks.

WHAT IS A MONOTREME?

Although mammals, monotremes share many characteristics with reptiles—their hipbone structures are similar to those of lizards, they lay eggs, their right and left oviducts are separate and not united to form a uterus, and they have a single urogenital opening called a cloaca. This single opening, or "monotreme," is the feature that gives them their name. The opening is used for the elimination of both liquid and solid wastes as well as for reproductive functions. Despite this, they are mammals—they nurse their young and have fur. Another peculiar characteristic is that they have no true teeth.

The short-nosed echidna (left) *is found in New Guinea, Tasmania, and Australia. The long-nosed echidna* (above) *is found only in New Guinea.*

allow them to operate as powerful diggers when searching for food, or to escape from danger. The males of both echidna species have a venom gland and spur on each hind leg, but the venom gland does not function. The long-nosed echidna is the larger of the species. It has five digits on each of its feet, but claws are present only on the middle three digits of its hind feet.

The short-nosed echidna has a round, compact body and closely packed spines on its back. At the end of its naked snout is a narrow, small mouth, through which it sticks its long, thin tongue to catch ants and other insects. It also has five digits on each foot, but in this case each digit has a claw. The claws on the second digits of the hind feet are much longer than the others and are twisted inward toward the central axis of the leg. This digit is the grooming toe, being able to reach down between the spines for grooming.

The spines of these animals are like enlarged hairs. They are yellow or white with a sharp black tip and are anchored in a thick layer of muscle in the skin. On the short-nosed echidna, the spines on the sides are round in cross section, but elsewhere on the body they are mixed with softer, flattened, smaller spines. The form of short-nosed echidna found on Tasmania is covered in a thick coat of brown hairs mixed with short spines on the back but longer and interlocked spines over its rear end. On all young long-nosed echidnas, the body is thickly covered with hair and small, short spines, but as the animals age, they may lose almost all of the hair and the spines over their back and flanks.

WHEN BRITISH ZOOLOGISTS FIRST SAW A PLATYPUS, THEY THOUGHT SOMEONE HAD STITCHED A BEAK ONTO AN OTTER'S BODY

Echidnas have small, bulging eyes. Their vision is probably not important in detecting food or danger in their natural habitat. They rely on their hearing to detect other animals or people approaching.

AUSTRALASIAN ISOLATION

The Australasian home of the platypus and echidnas, which includes New Guinea, is one of the most individual of all the zoogeographical zones of the world because its animal population consists of the unique indigenous (special to the area) order Monotremata and the majority of the world's marsupials. As a result of its isolation since the Cretaceous period, the placental mammals, such as wildcats and dogs, have not colonized it on a large scale. So the mammal population now existing in the region results largely from adaptation by the original species. These species are specialized to cope with a variety of local living conditions or ecological niches, and the strange monotreme order's survival has probably been partly due to the area's isolation from the animals of other continents.

All illustrations Mike Donnelly/Wildlife Art Agency

ANCESTORS

Scientists are not sure from what animals the monotremes are descended. They are mammals because they have fur and suckle their young, but they are also very similar to reptiles, including the ovoviviparous lizards (in which eggs are not laid but develop in the oviducts so that the young are born as free-living individuals). Some think that the monotremes may be descended from an ancestor of the reptiles and therefore have developed completely independently of the other mammals. The Cynodont *(left)* is a mammal-like reptile from which some of these scientists believe the monotremes are descended. It lived in the late Triassic period about 220 million years ago. Others claim that they are descended from the ancestors of the marsupials, the Pantotheres, that lived in the Jurassic period. There have been a few monotreme fossils found, in Australasia only. These have included Pleistocene materials, isolated lower molar teeth (from an animal named Obdurodon), and a single lower jaw with cross-crested molar teeth (from an animal named Steropodon) dating from about 120 million years ago. So either theory of monotreme origin is still possible.

THE MONOTREME'S FAMILY TREE

There is one species of platypus, or duckbill, and two species of echidnas, the long-nosed and the short-nosed. The long-nosed echidna is found only in New Guinea; the short-nosed echidna is found in New Guinea, Australia, and Tasmania. The platypus lives in eastern Australia and Tasmania.

PLATYPUS
Ornithorhynchus anatinus
(orn-ith-o-RINK-us an-AT-i-nus)

The platypus has often been described as an otter with a duck's beak. It is the only member of its family and has many unique features (see pages 1646 and 1647).

SHORT-NOSED ECHIDNA
Tachyglossus aculeatus (tack-ee-GLOSS-us ack-yoo-lee-AT-us)

The short-nosed echidna is the smallest of the two species. It has a compact, round body, closely set with spines. Its Latin genus name Tachyglossus means "swift tongue," which accurately describes the tongue's action as it rapidly catches food on its sticky surface. The tongue can extend up to 7 in (18 cm) from the tip of the snout.

LONG-NOSED ECHIDNA
Zaglossus bruijni (zag-LOSS-us bru-EE-nee)

The long-nosed echidna can be twice the size of its short-nosed relative, with a head-and-body length of up to 35 in (89 cm). Its Latin genus name Zaglossus means "mostly tongue."

MONOTREMATA

ANATOMY: THE PLATYPUS

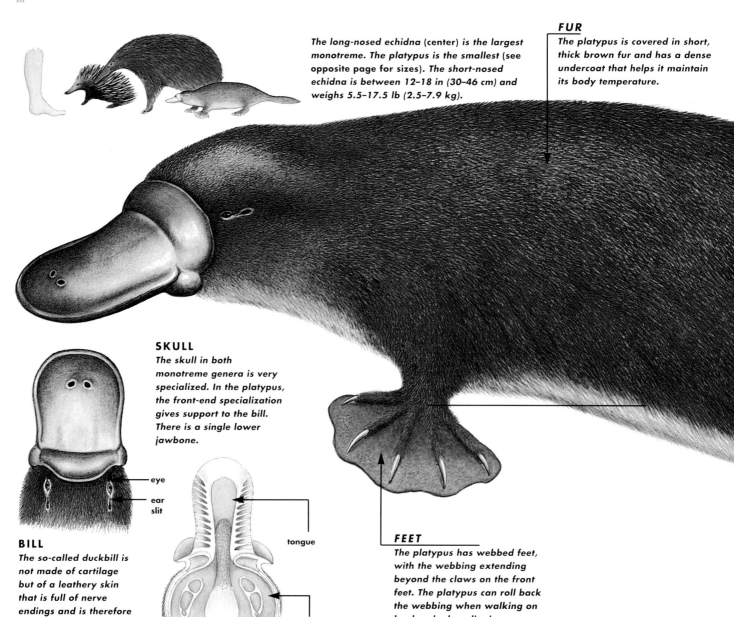

The long-nosed echidna (center) is the largest monotreme. The platypus is the smallest (see opposite page for sizes). The short-nosed echidna is between 12–18 in (30–46 cm) and weighs 5.5–17.5 lb (2.5–7.9 kg).

FUR

The platypus is covered in short, thick brown fur and has a dense undercoat that helps it maintain its body temperature.

SKULL

The skull in both monotreme genera is very specialized. In the platypus, the front-end specialization gives support to the bill. There is a single lower jawbone.

eye

ear
slit

tongue

cheek pouch

BILL

The so-called duckbill is not made of cartilage but of a leathery skin that is full of nerve endings and is therefore extremely sensitive.

FEET

The platypus has webbed feet, with the webbing extending beyond the claws on the front feet. The platypus can roll back the webbing when walking on land and when digging.

SKELETON

The hip and leg structure of the platypus is like that of lizards and crocodiles, not like other mammals. The legs splay out from the sides instead of support-ing the creature from underneath. The same is true for the echidna.

PLATYPUS
HIPBONE

epipubic bone

PLATYPUS
SKELETON

HIP

Another reptilian characteristic is the structure of the skeleton at the shoulder girdle and the presence of epipubic bones attached to the pelvic girdle (far left), which are bony extensions that presumably are partly for the support of the female's pouch.

X-ray illustrations Gary Martin/Wildlife Art Agency

muscle

gland

exposed poison
spur

reservoir

spur

foot

SPUR

The male platypus has horny spurs on the ankles of its hind legs that can deliver poison secreted by specialized poison glands. Only monotreme mammals have these spurs.

TAIL

The tail is used for storing fat, steering while swimming, and incubating eggs.

FACT FILE:

THE PLATYPUS

CLASSIFICATION

GENUS: *ORNITHORHYNCHUS*
SPECIES: *ANATINUS*

SIZE

HEAD–BODY LENGTH: MALE UP TO 24 IN (60 CM)
FEMALE UP TO 20 IN (50 CM)
TAIL LENGTH: 6–7.5 IN (15–19 CM)
WEIGHT/DIET: 2.2–4.8 LB (1–2 KG)/EATS INSECT
LARVAE, WORMS, CRUSTACEANS, TADPOLES
LIFESPAN: 10 TO 15 YEARS

COLORATION

DARK BROWN BACK, SILVER TO LIGHT BROWN
(SOMETIMES TINGED WITH PINK OR YELLOW)
UNDERSIDE WITH RUSTY BROWN MIDLINE,
ESPECIALLY IN YOUNG ANIMALS, WHICH HAVE
LIGHTEST FUR. FEMALES CAN BE IDENTIFIED BY A
MORE PRONOUNCED REDDISH TINT TO THEIR FUR

THE LONG-NOSED ECHIDNA

CLASSIFICATION

GENUS: *ZAGLOSSUS*
SPECIES: *BRUIJNI*

SIZE

HEAD–BODY LENGTH: 18–35 IN (46–89 CM)
TAIL LENGTH: VESTIGIAL TAIL
WEIGHT/DIET: UP TO 22 LB (10 KG)/EATS MAINLY
EARTHWORMS
LIFESPAN: ABOUT 15 YEARS IN THE WILD
(UP TO 30 YEARS IN CAPTIVITY)

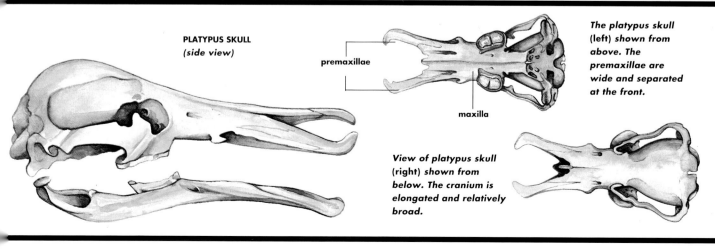

PLATYPUS SKULL
(side view)

premaxillae

maxilla

The platypus skull (left) shown from above. The premaxillae are wide and separated at the front.

View of platypus skull (right) shown from below. The cranium is elongated and relatively broad.

HIGHLY SPECIALIZED

ALTHOUGH MONOTREMES ARE FAIRLY ABUNDANT, THEY ARE RARELY SEEN. AS SOON AS THE SHORT-NOSED ECHIDNA SENSES DANGER, IT BURIES ITSELF SO FAST IT SEEMS TO BE SINKING IN QUICKSAND

The platypus is an active, largely crepuscular (confining most of its activities to early morning and late evening) animal. It shelters in burrows, which are dug in riverbanks. There are two types of burrows. One is used by both sexes as a shelter. During the mating season, however, the female moves out and builds a much larger and deeper burrow in which to give birth.

SOLITARY ECHIDNAS

Echidnas seem to be solitary creatures except when mating. They are very shy and, due to their good sense of hearing, they are also very alert. They run quickly, climb well, and scurry away from unusual

> THE PLATYPUS IS THE ONLY MAMMAL BESIDES CERTAIN SHREWS THAT IS VENOMOUS. THE POISON FROM ITS SPUR CAN KILL A DOG

noises, so, although they are quite common, they are rarely seen. The echidna walks with its legs fully extended so that its stomach is relatively high off the ground, and with its hind toes directed outward and backward it has a rather grotesque appearance when moving. Echidnas do not have a permanent shelter site but rest under piles of leaves, rubble, and brush, or in hollow logs. In wet forest with abundant food, an individual echidna's home range area, or territory, is about 120 acres (48.6 ha) and, with no obvious migration habits, this seems to change very little.

When threatened, the echidna first rolls itself into a ball, like a hedgehog, so that it is protected by its spines. Sometimes, in loose sandy soil, it uses its sharp claws to burrow rapidly down into the earth. It simply disappears, descending like an

elevator. Finally, all that is left is a little pile of dirt and a tuft of spines only about an inch (2–3 cm) high sticking out of the earth; looking like a tuft of grass, this provides effective camouflage. Alternatively, it might wedge itself into a crevice with its spines sticking out.

KEEPING WARM

On the whole, the monotremes are not as good as other mammals at controlling their body temperatures. The platypus tries to keep its body temperature relatively stable at about 89.6°F (32°C), which is low for a mammal. In some of its habitats the temperature can fall to around 40°F, and when it experiences these cold conditions it is able to increase its metabolic rate to generate the extra heat that maintains its correct body temperature. This is much warmer than that of reptiles in these cold conditions. Good fur and tissue insulation help the animal conserve body heat, and its

A long-nosed echidna forages for earthworms in the highland forests of New Guinea.

Jean-Paul Ferrero/Ardea

Des & Jen Bartlett/Survival Anglia

Baby echidnas are born naked and stay in the mother's pouch until the spines begin to grow.

burrow also offers shelter from extremes of temperature in both summer and winter.

Although echidnas are adaptable, they lack sweat glands and cope poorly with heat, dying quickly when exposed to temperatures above 95°F (35°C). They avoid these high temperatures by digging deep burrows and emerging only after dusk. Also, in order to maintain their water balance in arid regions, they select termites to eat in preference to ants because of their higher water content.

> THE PLATYPUS CAN LIVE IN ANY FRESHWATER—FROM ICY STREAMS AT OVER 5,000 FT (1,525 M) TO LAKES AND WARM COASTAL WATERS

In colder environments, echidnas become more active during the day and feed mainly on ants, which have a higher fat content than termites. Echidnas avoid the rain and will remain under cover and inactive for days if rain continues.

There are conflicting views about whether or not echidnas hibernate. However, since fhe mating season for some populations is midwinter, this is certainly not the case. The echidna overcomes the cold by storing up to 30 percent of its body weight as fat and by dropping its temperature to 10–12°F (5–6°C) below normal. In this state of torpor, the echidna can remain inactive for up to ten days. This allows it to survive periods of extreme cold.

An echidna (left) *burrows to hide from possible danger. Complete cover is achieved in seconds.*

Jean-Paul Ferrero/Ardea

HABITATS

Kathie Atkinson/Oxford Scientific Films

as well as on live termites. The termites build their nests underground or in dead wood—just where the echidna, which cannot tolerate very high temperatures, can find them.

Surrounding the outback and spread over much of the lowlands of Tasmania are areas of savanna and grassland. Climate in these areas ranges from seasonal wet and dry periods to Mediterranean and monsoon conditions. Termites are plentiful, and here species such as the compass or magnetic termite *(Amitermes meridionalis)* build their nests in the form of huge earth mounds that rise like tombs above the flat landscape. These wedge-shaped mounds are up to 11 ft (3.4 m) high and 10 ft (3 m) long but only about 3 ft (1 m) across. They usually point north/south with the broad sides facing east/west, so that they are mainly exposed to the cooler morning and evening

Short-nosed echidna (left) *on stony ground. In such a habitat the echidna rests and hides under rocks.*

The environments of Australasia are many and varied, ranging from the high equatorial mountains of New Guinea to the vast, dry desert of the Australian interior, which is popularly referred to as the outback. Echidnas have adapted to most of these environments.

The short-nosed species of echidna even survives in the heart of the outback, where the rainfall from the monsoons of New Guinea fails to reach inland, and the highlands in the east of the continent—the Great Dividing Range—act as a barrier to the moisture-bearing Pacific winds.

THE SHORT-NOSED ECHIDNA IS THE MOST WIDELY DISTRIBUTED OF ALL THE MONOTREMES

Here midday temperatures sometimes reach over 100°F (40°C) continuously for weeks on end and annual rainfall rarely exceeds 10 in (25 cm). In this harsh climate, vegetation is sparse, with low-growing acacia trees and species that have developed water-storing roots and flattened green stems instead of true leaves to minimize loss of water.

Mammals in the outback are few and far between, in terms of both numbers and variety of species, but there are rich supplies of termites and ants to be found, and these are the short-nosed echidna's main food. The termites feed on plant debris, and the ants on plant and animal remains,

The platypus lives in a wide range of temperatures, from near tropical to below freezing.

KEY FACTS

- Because the platypus is such a highly specialized mammal, particularly when it comes to feeding, any change to its habitat renders it vulnerable.

- Echidnas often sleep under rocks and in hollow logs, but they also dig burrows. If they are disturbed they roll into a ball like a hedgehog. When living in soft-soil areas, they burrow rapidly into the soil and cling to the sides by using their spines and claws.

- The platypus was once found in streams and rivers throughout eastern Australia, but hunting reduced its numbers. Now its numbers are increasing once more.

- The short-nosed echidna is a strong swimmer and will often cross water to reach a supply of food.

sun, and get the least sun at midday, when the sun's heat is fiercest, to keep the inside of the nest cool. The termites often top their mounds with tall, thin "chimneys" to ventilate the chambers deep within. The echidnas use their claws to dig into these nests for food. They also eat other species of termites, which forage for food in the open, providing easy pickings for the short-nosed echidnas.

Where ants and termites are plentiful, short-nosed echidnas do not roam far. Each has a living area of not more than 124 acres (50 ha), which is the equivalent of about 50 soccer fields. Within this area, the animal uses a variety of shelter sites. It usually feeds first thing in the morning and late in the afternoon, when it is less hot. During very hot periods it may feed only at night, spending the day in the shade of a clump of plants.

In New Guinea, echidnas are most plentiful in the central-highland forest regions, where the long-nosed, earthworm eating species is most prevalent.

DISTRIBUTION

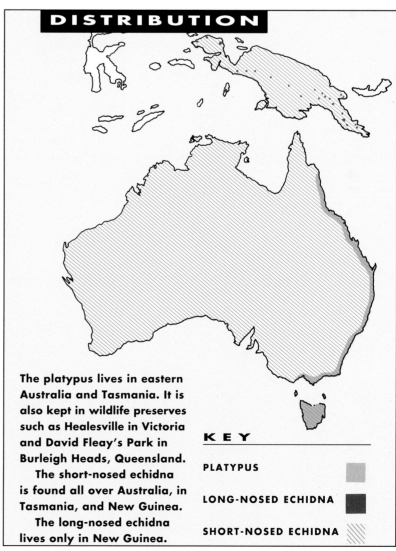

The platypus lives in eastern Australia and Tasmania. It is also kept in wildlife preserves such as Healesville in Victoria and David Fleay's Park in Burleigh Heads, Queensland. The short-nosed echidna is found all over Australia, in Tasmania, and New Guinea. The long-nosed echidna lives only in New Guinea.

KEY

PLATYPUS

LONG-NOSED ECHIDNA

SHORT-NOSED ECHIDNA

ANT/NHPA

With mountains reaching 14,000 ft (4,267 m) or more, the cooler climate of these regions, although variable, is always wet. Rainfall can average 400 in (1,016 cm) in a year and there can be frost and even snow on the highest peaks. The long-nosed echidna avoids any extremes of climate, and in cold conditions, or during long periods of rain, it enters a dormant state. Like the Australian echidnas, these long-nosed species have a living area that is smaller the more plentiful the food supply. Generally, this area is no more than 25 acres (10 ha).

The earthworms they eat are abundant in the soil of the forests, and some reach lengths of 10 ft (3 m) or more. They feed on leaves, which they pull into their burrows, or digest organic material in the soil or on its surface, thus helping to recycle nutrients and aerate the soil.

The short-nosed echidnas feed on ants within and beneath the forest floor. In these forest areas are other invertebrates including huge numbers of ants and termites—the ants generally being the more widespread. They mainly inhabit the forest floor, although leaf-cutter and weaving ants forage in the trees, where they are safe from the echidnas (which do not climb). The leaf-cutters dissect green leaves with their scissorlike mandibles and carry them back to their underground nests to eat. The weavers construct their nests by binding leaves

FOCUS ON

THE RIVERBANK WORLD OF THE TASMANIAN PLATYPUS

The duckbilled platypus is an Australian and Tasmanian original. It exists nowhere else in the world, looks and acts like nothing else, and in fact there was a time when it was not believed in anywhere else.

Separated from southeast Australia by the Bass Strait, Tasmania is the perfect setting for such an unusual animal. The island state is fortunate in having large areas almost empty of people. As a result, the government has been able to set aside about 30 percent of the land for national parks. These include the Western Tasmania National Parks Wilderness, a group of national parks that together form a World Heritage site. The wilderness covers 2,972 square miles (7,697 sq km) and contains rugged mountains, fast-flowing rivers, eucalyptus, and forests.

For the platypus of Tasmania, there is a plentiful supply of food in the clear waters. This is important to the platypus, because it probably needs more food relative to its body weight than any other mammal. Platypuses burrow extensively into riverbanks, usually leaving an entrance below water and another above.

TEMPERATURE AND RAINFALL

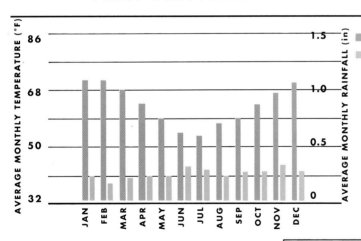

TEMPERATURE

RAINFALL

Australia is the world's largest country, but it is the smallest continent. Hobart, the capital of Tasmania, is a port with a population of 179,000. It is the coolest part of the island, with westerly winds blowing all year round.

together with strands of silk.

The world is divided into ten major biomes, or divisions of flora and fauna. Australasia is made up of six of these: tropical rain forest, desert, temperate grassland, savanna, scrub, and temperate rain forest. The short-nosed echidna is found in all of these contrasting regions. The long-nosed echidna lives only in tropical forests. The platypus can be found in regions of tropical and temperate forest and savanna.

NEIGHBORS

These animals coexist with the monotremes and depend on some of the same food supplies. They include marsupial mammal species, birds, and reptiles.

KOOKABURRA

The kookaburra has a noisy, laughing call that it uses to tell rivals to keep out of its territory.

TASMANIAN DEVIL

The Tasmanian devil will hunt prey but prefers carrion. As a result, it is not a threat to monotremes.

Illustrations T. A. Sitch/Wildlife Art Agency

TASMANIA

Tasmania is an island state of Australia lying to the southeast. It is the smallest state of the country and the least populous. Once called Van Diemen's Land, Tasmania has a flourishing tourist industry due to its natural beauty.

COPPERHEAD

Like the platypus, the copperhead eats frogs. It is usually coppery brown and about 5 ft long.

BLACK SWAN

About 3 ft long, both sexes have a pure black plumage, a red bill, and a trumpeting call.

WOMBAT

Like its relative the koala, the wombat looks like a small bear but is more like a badger in its habits.

NATIVE HEN

One of the 14 species of birds unique to Tasmania, the Tasmanian native hen is aquatic by nature.

QUOLL

This pouched mammal is arboreal and a carnivorous, nocturnal predator. Its jaws can open very wide.

FOOD AND FEEDING

The platypus is well adapted to its semiaquatic life and relies on its sensitive bill to locate food. Its bill, unlike that of a duck, is soft and flexible. The animal feels around with the bill, which is made of moist, sensitive, naked skin and is rich in nerve endings. It is unique among mammals for having no external ears; instead it has ear slits just above the eyes.

When diving, the platypus closes off its eyes and ear slits, which makes it blind and deaf under the water. This means that it relies on the tactile bill as an essential tool for locating prey. The nostrils, which are placed toward the end of the upper bill, only function when the head is in the air.

The platypus spends most of its time in freshwater and finds all its food there mainly at the bottom of rivers, lakes, and ponds. It makes dives that usually last a minute or more, probing the mud with its bill for small invertebrates such as shrimp, crayfish, and other crustaceans, as well as worms, tadpoles, larvae, and even small frogs. The food is scooped up in the bill and stored in special cheek pouches just behind the bill. Inside the pouches are horny ridges that help grind up the food into smaller pieces. There are also horny ridges in the bill and the mouth behind it.

The adult, unlike the young platypus, does not have any teeth, so it must grind its food against its palate using horny grinding plates at the back of its jaws. Its bill also has a horny ridge, which is used to demolish mollusk shells. Platypuses have enormous appetites, consuming up to 2.2 lb (1 kg) of food each night.

The legs of the platypus are short and powerful. Its webbed feet are adaptations to its watery home,

AMAZING FACTS

BIG EATER

In a single night, a platypus is able to eat its weight in food. In a zoo, a platypus ate 1,200 worms and 50 crayfish every 24 hours. It was once thought that the platypus was depriving trout of food. But studies have shown that although both feed on insect larvae, the trout prefers to eat swimming larvae, while the platypus feeds on bottom-dwelling species. Since the trout and the platypus are commonly found together, it is unlikely that they compete seriously.

in SIGHT

D. & E. Parer Cook/Ardea

USING ITS BILL

When it closes its eyes and ear slits to swim underwater, the platypus becomes virtually deaf and blind. It is able to find food and avoid obstacles by using its sensitive bill. There are some suggestions that it may sense electrical impulses generated in the water by its prey.

with the front feet being used to propel the animal through the water and the back ones for steering. When swimming, the platypus is very buoyant and floats high in the water. When diving for food, the end of each swimming stroke is pressed upward so that the body is forced down into the water. Out of the water, the webbing on the feet is rolled back to expose the claws, which are used for walking and digging.

Its fur is thick and short, another adaptation to its life in the water. The platypus also has a dense undercoat, which helps it maintain the correct body temperature.

SENSES

The bill is used to sense the presence of rocks and boulders and to locate food.

DIVING
Because it is so light and buoyant, the platypus forces itself to the bottom of the river by using the front feet.

FOOD

WATER SNAIL

TADPOLES

SHRIMP

CRAYFISH

KEY FACTS

● The platypus had an enormous impact on the scientific world when it was first discovered in 1796. Its ducklike bill, furry mammalian coat, and webbed feet appeared so strange to one scientist that he named it *paradoxus*.

● The platypus has virtually no long-standing, natural enemies, although a carpet-snake or goanna may occasionally catch one.

● After the platypus has collected its food from the bottom of the river, it returns to the surface to breathe and eat. It often returns to its burrow when leaving the water, reappearing moments later, dry and glossy. The sides of the burrow apparently squeeze the coat dry.

HUNTING

Echidnas are specialist feeders, hunting and foraging only for ants, termites, or worms. Some populations of short-nosed echidnas feed exclusively on ants, while other populations prefer a greater variety and include other insects and worms in their diet. In captivity the short-nosed echidna is partial to milk, eggs, bread, and other foodstuffs and thrives well on this "unnatural" diet.

The diet of the long-nosed echidna is even more restricted and is made up almost entirely of worms, which are abundant in this echidna's habitat of humid forests and alpine meadows.

Because of the different diets, the two species of echidnas have different types of tongues. However, in both species teeth are lacking, and the animals break up their food between horny ridges in their mouths.

LOCATING PREY

Smell plays a part in the selection of prey, but probably echidnas rely most on their remarkable collection of nerve receptors located on the tip of the snout, which is strong enough to be used to turn over the litter on the ground and even to break up soft logs in order to get to the ants and termites. The animals use the snout in preference to their strong claws in order to find food.

KEY FACTS

- The long-nosed echidna has hooks on its tongue, which it uses to eat worms. The hooks run in grooves in the tongue and the echidna has to hold the worm straight in order to maneuver it into its mouth.

- The snout of the long-nosed echidna accounts for two-thirds of the length of the echidna's head. It is curved downward.

- If the short-nosed echidna can find enough food throughout the year, it is able to withstand low temperatures and can avoid going into a torpor.

LOCATING ANTS
The echidna first uses its keen sense of smell to locate its meal of ants.

AMAZING FACTS

Alan Root/Survival Anglia

APPETITE FOR ANTS

The females of the ants that the short-nosed echidna hunts gain extra body fat during the early spring. At this time the echidna attacks the anthill directly, risking the stings of the ants to get at the fat-rich food.

Illustration Peter David Scott/Wildlife Art Agency

The tongue of the short-nosed echidna is up to 7 in (17.8 cm) long. Its mouth is only just big enough for it to move its tongue in and out to catch ants or termites. The long tongue is lubricated by a sticky saliva solution that makes the ants stick to it. This makes it very easy for the animal to eat large quantities of insects very quickly. It uses its outsized claws to tear open rotten logs while searching for ants and to break into the concrete-hard termite nests.

DIGGING

Once the ants have been located, the echidna roots them out using the tip of its snout.

D. & E. Parer Cook/Ardea

HOW THE LONG-NOSED ECHIDNA EATS WORMS

Worms are the principal diet of the long-nosed echidna. Their tongue is equipped with horny spines located in a groove that runs from the tip to about one-third of the way back. Worms are hooked by these spines when the tongue is extended. The long-nosed echidna has to learn to line up its prey either head or tail first so that it will slide easily into its very narrow mouth and along the tight channel that runs inside the snout to the alimentary canal in its body. It does this by using its forepaws to hold the earthworm while it positions its beak.

CATCHING ANTS

When the ants are finally exposed, the echidna catches them on its long, sticky tongue.

REPRODUCTION

The reproductive organs of the platypus and echidna are unique among mammals because they have only one urogenital (*uro* means excretion from the kidneys; *genital* has to do with reproduction) opening, the cloaca. This is why they are named monotremes, from the Greek meaning "one-holed creatures."

The animals dispose of undigested food and their waste products from the kidneys' urea through this external hole. Also, the male's sperm is ejected via this opening, as the penis is inside the body, and female monotremes deliver their eggs through the same hole.

The eggs of monotremes are larger than the (internal) eggs of other mammals, and the monotreme oviducts (egg channels) are two simple tubes, one on each side, which at their lower end

> WHEN THE FEMALE ECHIDNA LAYS AN EGG, SHE DEPOSITS IT INSIDE A SPECIAL POUCH. SCIENTISTS ARE NOT SURE EXACTLY HOW SHE DOES THIS

open into the cloaca. In addition, only the ovary and oviduct on the left side of the body are functional, as in birds, and the egg is fertilized in the part of the oviduct that corresponds to the placental's uterus. The female lays the egg after it is covered by a shell.

The testes of the male platypus and echidna are undescended and enclosed in the abdomen, a retained reptilian trait. The penis of the male is a groove made up of erectile tissue surrounding a sperm duct and is located in the cloacal floor. This tissue becomes enlarged and erect when filled with blood, so that it can be used during mating and inserted into the female's cloaca. This allows sperm to reach and fertilize the egg while it is still in the oviduct. The penis is used only for the passage of sperm; urine exits the male's cloaca via a separate urinary canal.

MATING ECHIDNAS

When female echidnas are ready to mate, they leave a scent trail that attracts the males. The only time echidnas are ever seen in groups is during mating, when sometimes several males can be seen following one female. Once they are pregnant, female echidnas dig a shallow burrow about 3–4.5 ft (1–1.4 m) long, where they lay a single egg.

The egg is placed in a backward-facing pouch that forms on her abdomen when she is breeding. The egg is coated with sticky mucus to help it stay in the pouch. It is kept in the pouch for seven to ten days until the infant hatches. The tiny echidna pokes through the shell using its egg tooth and a horny caruncle (a lump of hard flesh on its head).

The youngster suckles inside the pouch on the female's mammary glands, which turn inward instead of forming nipples.

BIRTH POUCH

In the breeding season, the female echidna grows an abdominal pouch when she is ready to lay an egg.

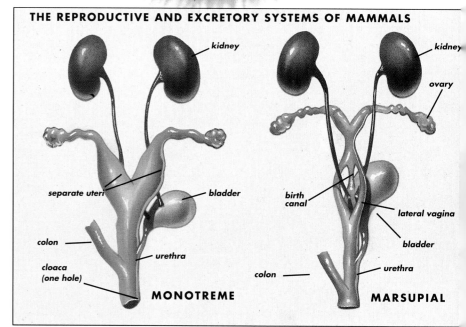

THE REPRODUCTIVE AND EXCRETORY SYSTEMS OF MAMMALS

MONOTREME: kidney, separate uteri, colon, cloaca (one hole), bladder, urethra

MARSUPIAL: kidney, ovary, birth canal, lateral vagina, bladder, colon, urethra

Illustrations Simon Roulstone

in SIGHT

ECHIDNA'S POUCH

The female echidna develops a breeding pouch only during the breeding season and when incubating an egg. It is a small, rearward-opening pouch that is retained only temporarily, being lost after the young echidna no longer needs its protection. This is when it has reached a weight of about 14 oz (400 g) and its spines begin to grow. The young continue to suckle for a further three to six months and become fully independent at about one year old.

Des & Jen Bartlett/Bruce Coleman Ltd.

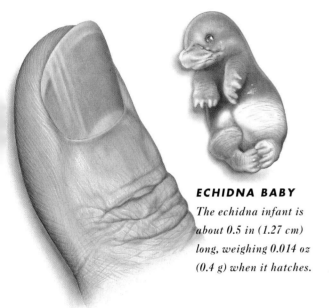

ECHIDNA BABY

The echidna infant is about 0.5 in (1.27 cm) long, weighing 0.014 oz (0.4 g) when it hatches.

GROWING UP

The baby begins to develop spines when it is between three and six weeks old. At six to eight weeks old it starts to become independent.

Illustrations Steve Kingston

There are three anatomical arrangements of the female urogenital systems in mammals: Monotremes have one hole, marsupials have two holes, and placental mammals have three holes, one each for the exits from the urinary, digestive, and reproductive systems.

kidney

ovary

vagina

bladder

urethra

colon

PLACENTAL MAMMAL

AMAZING FACTS

ALBINOS

Albino echidnas are a rare sight. Albinism occurs because of a congenital deficiency of coloring pigment in the skin, hair, and eyes. This means that the skin and hair are white and the eyes are pink. Albinism also occurs in plants lacking chlorophyll.

George Bingham/Bruce Coleman Ltd.

LIFE CYCLE

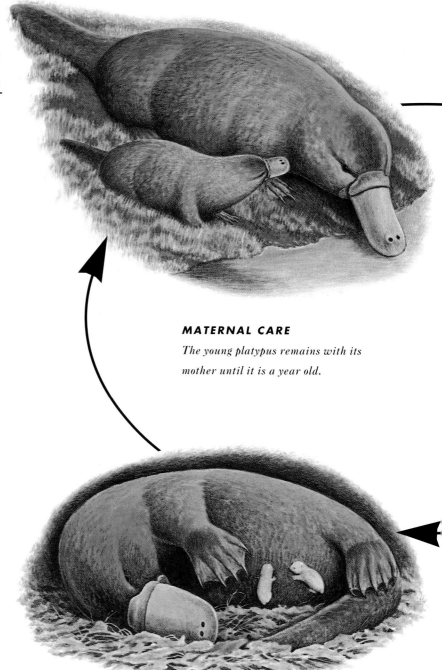

Platypuses mate in the water. First, the female slowly approaches the male. Then there is an elaborate courtship. The male chases the female, grasps her tail, and the two swim in circles before mating. Some days later the female goes off to start digging the long breeding burrow where she lays her eggs.

About two to four weeks after mating, usually between July and October (midwinter in Australasia), the female platypus lays two eggs in a nest at the end of her breeding tunnel, out of sight of any predators. The burrow is dug in a riverbank and is usually about 40–50 ft (12–15 m) long, with many branches to it. There may be more than one leaf-lined nesting chamber, and the female barricades herself in with piles of dirt and moist plant matter, which helps to keep the eggs from drying out during the incubation period.

The female probably lies on her back, curling her tail up to form a cup near the base of her belly, into which she rolls her two eggs. The leathery eggs are soft shelled, between 0.6–0.7 in (15–18 mm) in diameter, and are very sticky and probably cling to the mother's fur, as well as to each other, to keep

---

AFTER GIVING BIRTH, THE FEMALE PLATYPUS MAY STAY IN THE BURROW FOR UP TO FOURTEEN DAYS WITHOUT FEEDING UNTIL HER EGGS HAVE HATCHED

---

them from rolling out. As there is no brood pouch, the female broods and incubates the eggs by curling around them to keep them warm, holding them between her tail and abdomen for usually seven to ten days.

The baby platypuses, just about 0.5 in (12.7 mm) long on hatching, have another feature unique to monotreme mammals, but common in birds and reptiles. This is a temporary egg tooth with which to cut their exit from the egg. When the young are born they have hardly any bill, but they instead have lips. A few days after the young hatch, the mother begins to secrete milk from her mammary glands. The female platypus has no teats or nipples, and the milk is actually delivered from the mammary glands through the equivalent of sweat glands. These ducts from the mammary glands open into two long folds from which the young lick up the milk. The young also lick milk from the fur on the mother's abdomen.

The young have relatively large forelimbs for clinging to the fur, and they are very immature

MATERNAL CARE

The young platypus remains with its mother until it is a year old.

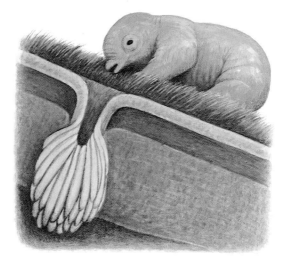

SUCKLING

The tiny youngsters suckle milk that is produced by the mother's mammary glands. Since she has no nipples, the milk oozes out onto her skin and fur, and the infants suck it up from there.

All illustrations Simon Turvey

GROWING UP

The life of a young platypus

PARENTAL CARE

In mammals, the sex involved most often in parental care is the female, since she is the one that can provide nourishment. The involvement of the male is rare, and in all monotremes parental care seems to be given by the female.

The females feed their young on milk after they hatch. The young echidna remains in the pouch until it becomes so large that it has to stay in a nest. The mothers return to the nest at intervals to suckle their offspring. Neither the young platypus nor the echidna is allowed to leave the nest until it is self-sufficient and able to protect itself to some extent.

THE EGGS

The female platypus normally lays two eggs in a nest in her long burrow. She broods them for seven to ten days, between her abdomen and tail. The infant platypus breaks out of its egg using its special egg tooth.

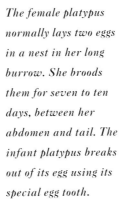

when they are born. They continue to suckle milk for a long time, not being weaned until they are four to six months old. They are then about 12–13.5 in (30–34 cm) long and able to take their first swim—they emerge from the nest and burrow in late summer (January to early March in New South Wales). They stay with their mothers until they are one year old. The fathers do not seem to be involved in caring for the young platypuses.

Females start to breed at two years of age but they do not breed every year. They take good care of the few young that they produce, and this seems to mean that they have a high survival rate, in spite of their low reproductive rate.

THE PLATYPUS BURROW

A mother platypus digs an extralong breeding burrow, sometimes up to 65 ft (20 m) long. The platypus uses its burrow to help it regulate its temperature in the extremes of the Australian climate. But, as mammals, they are able to regulate their body temperature to a reasonable extent. The female platypus makes a nest of leaves and grass for her eggs. When she goes into the burrow, she piles up dirt to block the entrance. Each time she enters or exits the burrow, she rebuilds her blockade. The mother does not leave the nest until the eggs are hatched. The male is excluded from the nursery burrow.

SAFE IN OUR HANDS?

ALTHOUGH NO LONGER IN DANGER OF EXTINCTION, THE PLATYPUS HAS BEEN LISTED AS "POTENTIALLY VULNERABLE" BECAUSE OF CONTINUING HUMAN ENCROACHMENT INTO ITS SPECIALIZED HABITAT

Many of the world's animal species are in danger of extinction or are becoming rare, often as a direct result of human activity. To protect these species requires understanding of local human cultures, environmental economics, and government priorities, as well as knowledge of biological sciences. All animal species, and especially the endangered ones, are monitored by the International Union for the Conservation of Nature (IUCN). Their status is listed in its *Red Data Book* and other reports. There is also a commission within the IUCN called the Species Survival Commission (SSC) that works through its nearly one hundred specialist groups. These focus on species either threatened with extinction or of

---

THE LONG-NOSED ECHIDNA IS BEING HUNTED FOR FOOD—WHICH IS STRANGE BECAUSE ITS DIET OF ANTS MAKES IT TASTE OF FORMIC ACID

---

special importance to human welfare.

In 1992 the IUCN/SSC specialist group for monotremes published a report called "Australasian Marsupials and Monotremes—An Action Plan For Their Conservation." In this report, the platypus is listed as "potentially vulnerable" in its aquatic environment. This is mostly because its habitat of lakes and rivers is at risk due to encroachment by people for water management, leisure activities, and building projects. Its decline in geographic range since European settlement some two hundred years ago is less than 10 percent, but the platypus is more vulnerable in South Australia than in Tasmania. It is now protected by law and are quite common in some areas, so are no longer in danger of extinction.

The Tachyglossus, or short-nosed echidna, is listed

as stable. The decline of its geographic range since European settlement is also less than 10 percent. Although it is hardly ever seen, the short-nosed echidna is not rare and in some areas is thriving.

The population of Zaglossus, or long-nosed echidnas in New Guinea and Indonesia is listed as vulnerable and has been declining because of forest clearance and overhunting. The animal needs careful protection to restore its numbers. The decline of its geographic range is between 50 percent and 90 percent since European settlement. It is protected by law in Indonesia, within a protected area system.

THE FUTURE

The platypus will thrive if its aquatic habitat is conserved or improved. This will require management of the appropriate lakes and rivers in a way that is compatible with the well-being of the

An example of the devastation caused by logging companies in Papua New Guinea (right).

Don Hadden/APSNZ/Ardea

The long-nosed echidna (above) *is the most vulnerable of all monotremes.*

Gary Bell/Planet Earth Pictures

THEN & NOW

This map shows the distribution of monotremes in Australasia. On a worldwide scale, their distribution has hardly changed over thousands of years. They have been found only in Australasia.

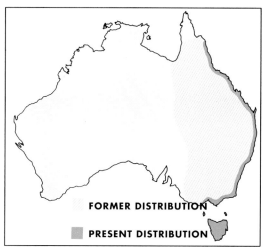

FORMER DISTRIBUTION

PRESENT DISTRIBUTION

The western limits of the platypus are the Leichardt River in North Queensland and the Murray Onkaparinga and Glenelg Rivers, just within the border of South Australia. On the local scale in the area shown above, there has been a distinct reduction in numbers and distribution over the last two hundred years, since man and other species have encroached on the monotremes' natural territory. Although exact figures have not been readily available, it is clear that the platypus came close to extinction even though its geographic range has not shrunk more than 10 percent since European settlement. Now its numbers are recovering well, in the same areas as before.

The short-nosed echidna's geographic spread has probably not shrunk relatively any more than that of the platypus, but its numbers have not been reduced in the same way. It is therefore the most stable "then and now."

The long-nosed echidna has become the most vulnerable monotreme, with its population quite severely depleted and its geographic range having seen a steep decline of between 50 and 90 percent since European settlement. While some environmental improvements are taking place, its numbers are not yet recovering sufficiently.

ZEFA

In the 19th century, fur hunting was a popular sport. The platypus's thick molelike fur was much prized and the animal was hunted nearly to extinction. Once this hunting was stopped, its numbers increased, and it is now in no danger. Unfortunately the same cannot be said for the long-nosed echidna. This is still being hunted, mainly for sport but also for food. All three monotremes have probably been able to survive because they are highly specialized for their habitat.

Ford Kristo/PEP

The duckbilled platypus (above) is highly susceptible to changes in habitat.

A researcher (left) gently handles a juvenile platypus. Conservationists have worked hard to ensure a future for platypuses.

Many platypuses have fallen afoul of fishing nets (below).

animal. The problems are well understood and there seems to be a favorable approach by the Australian government and all the relevant wildlife authorities.

The platypus owes its recent success to its occupation of an ecological niche that has been long-lasting, even on the driest continent. On the other hand, the platypus is a highly specialized mammal and is very susceptible to the effects of changes in habitat. So far, the impact of man's damage to the environment has only affected individual platypus populations. Care and proper action must be taken in order to maintain this unique species.

The long-nosed echidna is likely to thrive only if the traditional view of the animal as a highly prized game species can be changed. It is this traditional hunting by humans that has caused part of its decline. The change will need hard work by local governments and responsible wildlife authorities. ■

in SIGHT

Although the platypus is rigidly protected, it still falls afoul of wire cages that have been set underwater to catch fish. Should the platypus enter one, it cannot escape and drowns, because it is not able to stay underwater for much longer than five minutes.

The platypus is also indirectly under threat from rabbits. In areas where the rabbits have dug too many tunnels, the platypus cannot breed, because it needs undisturbed soil for its breeding burrows.

Another threat comes from the twelve million or so feral cats that prey on hundreds of native species of monotremes, marsupials, birds, and reptiles.

Jus Kiely/NHPA

INTO THE FUTURE

The platypus has a very specialized habitat in that it must live alongside freshwater rivers and lakes. This aquatic habitat must be protected from the encroachment of man, and from other burrowing animals such as the rabbit, if this wonderful animal is to survive. At the moment, however, it is apparently in no extreme danger.

HUNTING THREAT

The long-nosed echidna is hunted for human food by the natives of Papua New Guinea; it has become scarce because of this and the deforestation of its natural habitat, which is caused chiefly by logging. However, it is now protected by law in both Irian Jaya (a province of Indonesia) and Papua New Guinea, although this does not stop all the traditional hunting. The short-nosed echidna seems to be the least affected of the monotreme species and is thriving in most of its natural habitat.

PREDICTION

HOPE FOR THE LONG-NOSED ECHIDNAS

Platypuses have benefited from measures designed to cut down hunting, and the same will hopefully happen with the Zaglossus, which are listed as "vulnerable" in New Guinea and Indonesia.

On the whole, the monotremes have a more assured future now than at any time over the past two hundred years, thanks to the work of conservation groups and to the improvements in the public's knowledge of these animals. However, it is vital that wildlife conservation groups keep informing the public and government bodies of the continuing risks to the platypus to ensure that this fascinating animal does not once again suffer from human complacency. ∎

PREDICTION

MORE PRIVATE PRESERVES

It is clear that endangered species such as platypuses can be protected from native predators in private preserves, so it is likely that more examples of these protected areas will be set up in the future.

PROTECTED AREAS

Some private companies are starting to build wildlife sanctuaries that will keep native predators such as foxes and wildcats away from the endangered species. These sanctuaries, which are being funded by capital raised through selling shares to the public, are beginning to compete with the national wildlife parks. Such companies feel that some new conservation ideas are desperately needed, and they obviously see an opportunity to profit from offering the public more exciting places to observe the rare species. These species include, among others, platypuses, bandicoots, and bettongs.

Another vital conservation measure includes trying to breed the species in captivity and then releasing the offspring back to the wild.

Alan Root/Survival Anglia

Illustration Evi Antoniou

POLAR BEARS

RELATIONS

Polar bears belong to the bear family, or Ursidae. Other members of this family include:

GRIZZLY BEAR

BLACK BEARS

SUN BEAR

SPECTACLED BEAR

SLOTH BEAR

PANDA

Tim Walker/ZEFA-Allstock

POLAR PREDATORS

SYMBOL OF THE FAR NORTH, THE HUGE AND POWERFUL POLAR BEAR ENDURES FIERCE BLIZZARDS AND BITTER COLD IN THE VAST ARCTIC WILDERNESS

M uch of a polar bear's life is spent in the constant night of the long Arctic winter or in the twilight of the spring and autumn. The snow reflects what little light there is. It's a dark, barren world, periodically illuminated by moonlight and the beautiful displays of the northern lights.

Among the world's largest carnivorous land mammals, polar bears are about ten times the size of humans, with large males weighing over 1,540 pounds (700 kilograms). Each of their great paws may measure 12 inches (30 centimeters) across and is armed with five large, curved claws.

Polar bears move faster in snow than any other animal, though they also spend a good deal of time in the water; their scientific name *Ursus maritimus* (UR-suss mar-IT-tee-muss) means "sea bear." The long neck and small head, with its smooth profile, give them a streamlined shape, and they are naturally buoyant because of their thick layer of

CLASSIFICATION

Polar bears belong to a group of meat-eating mammals called carnivores. All bears are closely related to dogs and belong to the super-family Canoidea, or doglike animals. The bear family contains eight species, which are divided into three genera. The polar bear is one of three species belonging to the subfamily Ursinae.

CLASS
Mammalia
(mammals)

ORDER
Carnivora
(carnivores)

SUBORDER
Fissipedia
(land-living carnivores)

SUPERFAMILY
Canoidea
(doglike forms)

FAMILY
Ursidae
(all bears)

SUBFAMILY
Ursinae

GENUS
Ursus

SPECIES
maritimus

body fat. Other adaptations for swimming are their partly webbed feet and strong legs.

Polar bears swim using their front paws, allowing their hind legs to float out behind them. Sometimes they hold their hind legs together to form a rudder, with which they steer. They can swim up to 6 miles (10 kilometers) an hour and can go nonstop for 100 miles (160 kilometers).

When they dive under water, polar bears flatten their ears but keep their eyes open, and they can remain submerged for up to two minutes. A reflex action ensures that their nostrils close and, at the same time, their heartbeat slows down and their muscle cells switch to functioning without oxygen.

LIVING IN ONE OF THE WORLD'S MOST EXTREME ENVIRONMENTS, THE POLAR BEAR HAS ADAPTED TO SURVIVE INTENSE COLD AND BITTER WINDS

The polar bear has adapted in a number of ways to its harsh environment. Its large muzzle contains a complex network of heat-exchanging passages in which its exhaled breath warms up the ice-cold air before it enters the animal's lungs. Its thick coat of creamy-white fur, its tough black skin, and a layer of stored fat, or blubber, provide excellent insulation.

The long outer guard hairs of its fur coat are hollow, their whiteness caused by the tiny air cavities within them. They funnel much of the sunlight through them to reach the skin. Being black, the skin absorbs a good deal of warmth.

In the water, where the polar bear's fur cannot

Dan Guravitch/ZEFA-Allstock

Art Wolfe /ZEFA-Allstock

A mother and cub cool off in the icy Arctic waters (above), *before they set off again in the never-ending search for food in a harsh climate* (right).

This family group makes the most of scant resources as they devour the remains of a walrus.

Nikita Ovsyanikov/Planet Earth Pictures

provide insulation, its thick layer of blubber prevents the animal from becoming dangerously chilled. After swimming, the bear will shake itself vigorously like a dog to dry off; its coat sheds water easily.

In fact, the polar bear retains heat so well that it can easily become overheated. Old males in particular, with their huge layer of blubber, overheat very quickly when they run, even in the bitterest cold. Experiments conducted on polar bears walking on a treadmill have shown that even at air temperatures as low as -12°F (-25°C), walking at a mere 4.5 miles (7 kilometers) an hour, their body temperature soared to 100°F (39°C).

For bioenergetic reasons, polar bears rarely hunt fast-moving prey, as the energy costs are likely to be greater than the energy obtained from the prey. To help deal with the problem of overheating, polar bears have "hot spots" on the ears, muzzle, nose, footpads, and the inside of the thighs, where excess heat is lost. The bears also cool off by swimming, as water conducts heat about twenty times better than air.

EARLY SETTLERS

Compared with most other carnivores, bears evolved relatively recently—about 25 million years ago—rising from the same stock as early dogs. Discoveries of fossils have shown that bears first appeared in Europe about 20 million years ago and subsequently spread throughout much of the world, except for Australia and Antarctica.

The earliest known fossil bear, aptly named the dawn bear, was only the size of a fox and had a chiefly carnivorous diet. Over millions of years and as different species evolved, the skull grew larger and the teeth developed as bears changed from a carnivorous to an omnivorous diet, where their menu included plants, fruit, and insects as well as meat. The carnassials became smaller or disappeared, and the molars became broad and flat with rounded cusps for crushing up tough plant food.

These more modern bears grew heavier, with very short tails and shorter limbs. Instead of running on their toes like dogs or cats, bears adopted a plantigrade movement, which means that they run with the entire sole of their foot on the ground.

NEW SURROUNDINGS

Polar bears are thought to have evolved from brown bears that switched from an omnivorous diet to specializing in catching seals on the sea ice. Able to take advantage of an abundance of food without competition from other carnivores, the ice-dwelling

> POLAR BEARS WERE THE MOST RECENT BEARS TO EVOLVE, FIRST APPEARING IN SIBERIA BETWEEN 300,000 AND 250,000 YEARS AGO

brown bears adapted to the cold and gradually a new species evolved.

These new bears developed a streamlined body and partly webbed feet for swimming, a thick coat and blubber for warmth, huge, furry feet for walking on ice, and sharper teeth and claws for killing their prey. Compared with those of other bears, their ears grew smaller and their tails shorter in order to conserve heat. Their necks became slimmer and longer so that they could reach into holes in the ice to catch seals. They had found their niche. ■

THE POLAR BEAR'S FAMILY TREE

Today there are eight species of bears, all descended from the now extinct dawn bear. They can be roughly divided into two groups. The first includes the polar bear and the brown or "grizzly" bear, while the second consists of the sun bear, the American and Asiatic black bears, and the sloth bear. The final members of the bear family are the spectacled bear and the giant panda, unique and famous as the symbol of the World Wide Fund for Nature.

BROWN BEAR

ASIAN BLACK BEAR

AMERICAN BLACK BEAR

GIANT PANDA

SPECTACLED BEAR

DAWN BEAR

Illustrations Barry Croucher/Wildlife Art Agency

POLAR BEAR

Ursus maritimus

(UR-suss mar-IT-tee-muss)

The polar bear and the brown bear share a common ancestor known as Ursus etruscus (UR-suss ee-TRUSS-kuss). The polar bear differs from the brown bear in being slightly bigger and in its specialist adaptations to its extreme habitat: for example, its white coat, its strong swimming ability, and its more streamlined shape.

SUN BEAR

SLOTH BEAR

ANCESTORS

In Europe, at the height of the last great Ice Age, there lived an impressive creature called the cave bear, *Ursus spelaeus* (UR-suss spell-AY-us). It may have measured as much as 8 feet (2.5 meters) long and weighed more than 1,500 pounds (680 kilograms). Like the modern brown bear, it escaped the harsh winters by hibernating in alpine caves.

Huge heaps of fossil bones have been found in these caves—the Dragon's Cave in Austria contained the remains of over 30,000 cave bears. Despite their great size and formidable appearance, cave bears were probably largely vegetarian. They may have survived until as recently as 35,000 years ago, when they were hunted by early humans armed with flint spears.

ANATOMY:
THE POLAR BEAR

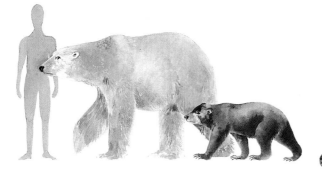

LONG NECK

Polar bears have longer necks than other bears, making them streamlined for swimming.

The polar bear is the largest living land carnivore. Males reach up to 5 ft (1.6 m) at the shoulder. In comparison, the sun bear of Southeast Asia, which is the smallest member of the bear family, reaches a maximum height of only 2.3 ft (70 cm), about the length of a polar bear's legs.

BROWN BEAR

Compared to the polar bear, the brown or grizzly bear has a much larger head, with a broader face and prominent muzzle.

BLACK BEAR

Otherwise similar in appearance to the brown bear, the American black bear has a narrower head and face and a shorter, sleeker coat.

THE NOSE

Polar bears have an extraordinary sense of smell, essential in such a barren environment. It is estimated that they can smell the carcass of a whale or a seal from as far away as 20 miles (32 km).

The polar bear's claws are protected by thick fur padding, which provides traction as it walks, while the brown bear's longer claws dig in the ground.

POLAR BEAR   BROWN BEAR

Illustrations Barry Croucher/Wildlife Art Agency

X
RAY

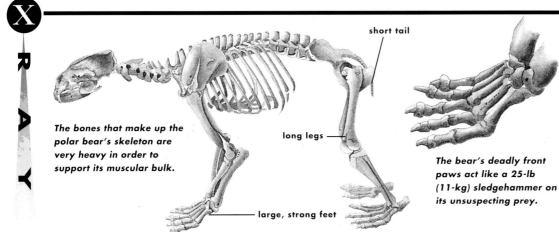

The bones that make up the polar bear's skeleton are very heavy in order to support its muscular bulk.

short tail

long legs

large, strong feet

The bear's deadly front paws act like a 25-lb (11-kg) sledgehammer on its unsuspecting prey.

Short but extremely sharp claws are perfect for holding on to a slippery seal.

X-ray illustrations Elisabeth Smith

Despite appearances, a polar bear's skin is, in fact, black. The bear looks white because its fur is made up of hollow hairs that reflect the sun. Beneath its skin lies a layer of fat that keeps the bear warm in the coldest Arctic winters.

hollow hairs

black skin

fat

CROSS SECTION OF SKIN AND HAIR

CLASSIFICATION

GENUS: *URSUS*

SPECIES: *MARITIMUS*

SIZE

HEAD–BODY LENGTH/MALE: **8–10 FT (2.5–3 M)**

HEAD–BODY LENGTH/FEMALE: **6.5–8 FT (2–2.5 M)**

SHOULDER HEIGHT/MALE: **5 FT (1.6 M)**

WEIGHT/MALE: **770–1,540 LB (350–700 KG)**

WEIGHT/FEMALE: **330–1,000 LB (150–450 KG)**

WEIGHT AT BIRTH: **1–1.5 LB (500–700 G)**

COLORATION

VARIES FROM PURE WHITE IN CUBS TO BLUISH WHITE, CREAMY WHITE, OR YELLOWISH IN ADULTS (THE YELLOW COLOR MAY BE CAUSED BY THE OXIDATION OF SEA OIL)

FEATURES

HUGE PAWS UP TO **12 IN (30 CM)** ACROSS

POWERFUL, STREAMLINED BODY

BLACK SKIN BENEATH FUR

DARK EYES AND A BLACK NOSE

EXTREMELY SHARP CLAWS

STRONG LEGS

The polar bear's long, square legs need to be very strong to support such bulk. They enable the bear to cover huge distances (up to 700 miles/1,200 km a year) in its endless search for prey.

HUGE STOMACH

Because of the scarcity of prey in the Arctic, the polar bear must make the most of every meal. The stomach of an adult male can expand to take up to 220 lb (90 kg) of meat and blubber in one sitting.

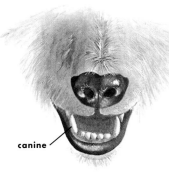

canine

The polar bear's long canine teeth show it to be a true carnivore, the only bear almost wholly dependent on meat. Most bears tend to be largely omnivorous, but the polar bear's diet of seal meat has resulted in the evolution of carnassial, or flesh-shearing, teeth, a feature undeveloped in the other bears.

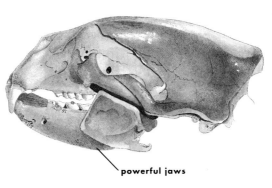

powerful jaws

Although the polar bear's powerful jaws are typical of a hunter, they are not actually used to kill prey; this duty is performed by a heavy blow from the bear's awesome paws. The jaws are used to pull victims from the water. In the case of such prey as beluga whales, this is quite some task.

AGAINST ALL ODDS

THE WORLD'S LARGEST LAND PREDATOR, THE POLAR BEAR IS A PATIENT, RESOURCEFUL HUNTER, OFTEN ROAMING VAST DISTANCES IN SEARCH OF FOOD

Superbly adapted to its harsh environment, the polar bear is at the top of the High Arctic food chain. The most carnivorous of all bears, feeding mainly on seals, polar bears travel great distances across their icy realm. They are the most northerly of all mammals and polar bear tracks and droppings have been found within a few miles of the North Pole itself.

It was long thought that polar bears spent their lives wandering at random through the Arctic, but, by radio tracking, it has been discovered that most polar bears remain in the same general area from year to year, moving around within it as the ice shifts with the seasons. This home range may be

These young polar bears are play-fighting in their territory of Hudson Bay, Canada. Real fights are comparatively rare, except during the mating season when adult males fight over females. At all other times, smaller bears simply avoid or flee from larger ones.

Art Wolfe/ZEFA-Allstock

relatively small in areas where the ice is more stable, and allows the bear regular access to areas where it can hunt seals. In other regions such as the Barents, Greenland, or Bering Seas, a bear may have to travel hundreds of miles each year to follow the shifting ice, and home ranges can be as large as 100,000 square miles (260,000 square kilometers).

Polar bears spend much of their time asleep or resting (above) to conserve energy, though they do not hibernate.

Polar bears sometimes travel many hundreds of miles every year.

Bryan and Cherry Alexander

Jeff Foott/Auscape International

Just how the bears manage to navigate around such huge areas remains a mystery. Researchers believe that young bears learn the seasonal pattern of movements during the two and a half years or more they accompany their mothers.

Except for females and their cubs, polar bears normally avoid one another except when mating or

---

POLAR BEARS' INTENSE CURIOSITY CAN LEAD THEM INTO HUMAN ENVIRONMENTS AND EVEN INTO CONFLICT WITH MAN

---

when they gather together at places where food is plentiful. Leading solitary lives, they have a limited vocabulary and relatively few facial expressions. Polar bears living in open country make very few calls. Threatening males make quiet coughing sounds, called chuffing, and cubs and their mothers keep in touch by braying or moaning.

Polar bears spend a good deal of their time asleep to conserve energy. A polar bear is capable of sleeping in any position, using a block of ice as a pillow or lying in drifting snow until its body is completely covered. They often relax in "daybeds"— hollows created by scooping out snow—adopting different postures either to lose heat or to conserve it. On warm days, they sprawl, even lying on their backs with their feet in the air; in cold weather they curl up. When there is a shortage of food or a female is nursing in the den, polar bears can survive on the fat stores in their bodies, but they do not hibernate.

Polar bears have an intense natural curiosity that can lead them into conflict with their only real rival, humans. As well as falling victim to native Inuit hunters, polar bears are sometimes shot after injuring or killing people they encounter when they visit towns or land fills.   ■

1675

HABITATS

Despite their name, polar bears rarely visit the North Pole itself, although they are found throughout the arctic regions, particularly on the Arctic Ocean pack ice—thick and heavily ridged ice—and along the surrounding coasts. Individual bears have even ended up as far south as Iceland, northern Japan, and Newfoundland, Canada.

The Arctic can be a stunningly beautiful place. In summer, the intense blue of the sky contrasts dramatically with the dazzling white of the vast expanses of ice and snow. In the clear air, the only sounds to break the silence over this great wilderness may be the rushing of a distant river or the occasional eerie howls of a wolf pack. The word *Arctic* comes from *arktos* (ARK-toss), the Greek name for "bear," because it is the land where the constellation of Ursa Major, the Great Bear, shines

Johnny Johnson/Bruce Coleman Ltd.

Bryan and Cherry Alexander

Well adapted to its harsh environment, the polar bear can weather almost any storm. Its thick coat and layer of insulating fat protect it from the cold.

At the mercy of the winds and sea currents, this polar bear (left) is following the shifting pack ice as it melts, breaks up, and refreezes.

brightly in the night sky directly above.

The Arctic is a frozen ocean encircled by the northern fringes of the continents of Europe, Asia, and North America and the island of Greenland. Here, animals have adapted over the slow process of evolution to a harsh world of ice, rock, and permanently frozen soil. In summer, the pack ice covers about 45 percent of the ocean, over 2 million square miles (about 6.6 million square kilometers); it covers more than 85 percent in winter.

ALTHOUGH IT LOOKS LIKE LAND COVERED WITH SNOW AND ICE, THE ARCTIC IS ACTUALLY A FROZEN OCEAN, BORDERED WITH FRINGES OF LAND

During the grim Arctic winter, when temperatures plummet to below -40°F (-40°C), the sun remains below the horizon for months on end, and the only source of heat is the inflow of air from lower latitudes. Even during the summer, the sun never rises far above the horizon and brings little heat—the average highest temperature does not exceed 50°F (10°C)—though slopes facing the sun

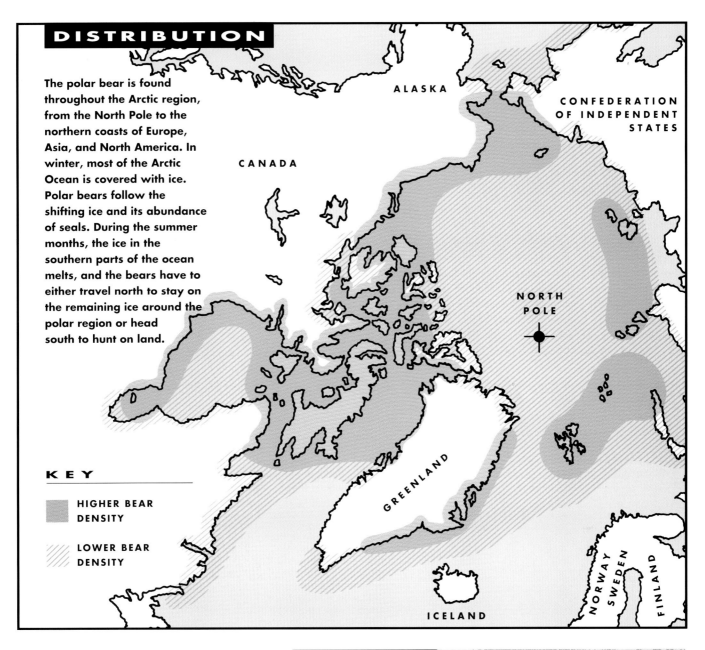

DISTRIBUTION

The polar bear is found throughout the Arctic region, from the North Pole to the northern coasts of Europe, Asia, and North America. In winter, most of the Arctic Ocean is covered with ice. Polar bears follow the shifting ice and its abundance of seals. During the summer months, the ice in the southern parts of the ocean melts, and the bears have to either travel north to stay on the remaining ice around the polar region or head south to hunt on land.

KEY

HIGHER BEAR DENSITY

LOWER BEAR DENSITY

ALASKA

CONFEDERATION OF INDEPENDENT STATES

CANADA

NORTH POLE

GREENLAND

NORWAY SWEDEN FINLAND

ICELAND

can be surprisingly warm. Polar bears in more northerly areas—both males and females—may dig out dens in the snow in winter to survive the fierce blizzards and bitter cold.

In the Arctic region, the great northern conifer forests gradually give way to the vast open spaces of the tundra. Though the tundra is dotted with lakes, ponds, and winding rivers, chill winds and a covering of snow and ice for much of the year allow only very hardy, stunted plants to grow.

The life of the polar bear is one of adjustment to a constantly changing environment and a moving food source. Winds keep the pack ice in almost constant motion in a giant clockwise spiral—it may travel up to 50 miles (80 kilometers) a day. This eternal drifting means that, to stay in one feeding area, polar bears must compensate for

KEY FACTS

● The Arctic is a frozen ocean encircled by Europe, Asia, North America, and Greenland. It stretches for over 5 million square miles (almost 15 million square kilometers).

● Despite their name, polar bears rarely visit the North Pole itself, as much of the polar basin is covered by thick ice built up over several years and there is not much to eat there.

● In winter, when howling winds and fierce blizzards add to the icy chill, Arctic temperatures may plummet to below -40°F (-40°C). Even summer temperatures do not rise above 50°F (10°C).

● Floating ice packs, pushed along by winds and currents, may travel as much as 50 miles (80 kilometers) a day.

the drift by moving in the opposite direction. How they do this in an environment devoid of landmarks remains a mystery.

Winds and currents also break up the ice to form long stretches of open water called leads. Such areas are important to polar bears because seals, the bears' main prey, are more abundant there. The bears also use systems of leads as migration routes.

HIDDEN DEPTHS

Pressure ridges, which are usually found along coastlines, in fjords, and in large bays containing islands, are formed when areas of ice are forced together. They may snake across the ice for many miles. In areas where snow can accumulate in drifts along these ridges, ringed seals make breathing holes in the ice. Here, in spring, the female seals dig out lairs in which to give birth to their pups. Polar bears, particularly females with young cubs, are attracted by this supply of food.

The bears are forced to move as the ice shifts, breaks up, and refreezes. In some places, such as the Greenland and Bering Seas, their distribution changes dramatically over the course of the year. In other areas to the south, notably the Hudson and James Bays, the ice melts completely in summer.

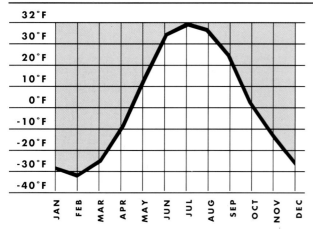

HIGH ARCTIC TEMPERATURES

This forces the bears ashore, where they remain, roaming inland into coniferous forests, until the winter comes and the sea refreezes; then they return to hunt seals again.

Although the salt in the seawater becomes trapped as the ice freezes, it gradually melts down through the ice, so that ice a year or more old is almost salt-free. This is an advantage to polar bears because they do not need to visit land for freshwater; they can drink from puddles that form as the surface of the ice melts. ∎

FOCUS ON

THE HIGH ARCTIC

To the north of, and overlapping, the tundra zone lies the High Arctic, where summer temperatures do not exceed 41°F (5°C) and only the most specialized plants and animals can survive. This is a world of stony or gravelly polar deserts and extensive areas of land buried by ice caps. The huge ice cap covering much of the interior of Greenland extends far to the south. In some places the flat Arctic landscape is broken by mountain ranges with peaks permanently covered in dazzling snow and ice.

With large areas devoid of land vegetation, the animals living in the High Arctic mostly depend, directly or indirectly, on the sea for their food. Food chains start with the simple organisms that drift passively with the ocean currents and are collectively known as plankton. The plant plankton is eaten by the animal plankton. Animal plankton, in turn, provides food for the great baleen whales, such as the bowhead whale. Arctic cod feed on both plant and animal plankton and are in turn eaten by other, larger fish. Fish are preyed on by various seabirds, seals, and toothed whales such as belugas and narwhals.

Land-based predators in the High Arctic include the wolf, Arctic fox, and stoat. At the top of the food chain, feeding almost entirely on seals on the ice and at the ice edge, is the polar bear. The killer whale is the top predator in the open sea, feeding on other whales as well as on fish and seals.

Although there is some seasonal variation in the climate of the High Arctic, temperatures rarely rise above 32°F (0°C). In the depths of winter, average temperatures are recorded as -33°F (-36°C), but on occasion they may plummet to as low as -40°F (-40°C). The relative warmth of late spring and summer promotes a new flush of vegetation.

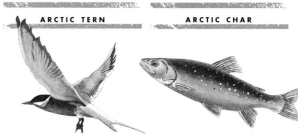

NEIGHBORS

These creatures coexist with the polar bear and other predators of the High Arctic, though some, such as the fox and the mosquito, are limited to the areas covered by tundra, not by ice.

ARCTIC TERN

This bird breeds in the Arctic and then migrates to spend the summer in the Antarctic. It feeds on fish and plankton.

ARCTIC CHAR

A member of the salmon family, this fish ranges around the whole of the High Arctic, returning to rivers to spawn.

Illustrations Elisabeth Smith

THE HIGH ARCTIC

The Arctic is roughly divided into three zones—Low, Middle, and High—according to the amount of plant life present. The Low Arctic has plenty of year-round vegetation; the Middle has some, usually in low-lying areas; whereas the High, where it is not covered by ice, is mostly rocky with scattered vegetation.

High Arctic

ENEMIES

KILLER WHALE

The ferocious killer whale eats mostly fish, seals, and whales but will seize the chance to attack an unsuspecting bear.

WALRUS

Weighing up to 1.5 tons (1.6 tonnes), the walrus is a powerful enemy, and its long tusks can be lethal weapons.

Illustrations Matt Lyon

MODERATELY DANGEROUS

MODERATELY DANGEROUS

Jeff Foott/Survival Anglia

SNOWY OWL

This owl feeds mainly on lemmings, and the number of young it produces depends on how well lemmings breed.

ARCTIC FOX

This wily predator hunts a variety of small prey. It has a dense white coat and can survive extreme cold.

GREENLAND SHARK

About 10 ft (3 m) long, this harmless shark swims slowly near the seabed and feeds on fish and crustaceans.

IVORY GULL

A year-round resident of the High Arctic, the ivory gull survives the winter by scavenging polar bear kills.

MOSQUITO

The mosquito is abundant in the Arctic summer, but spends most of the winter as a cold-resistant egg.

HUNTING

Their heightened senses and physical strength make polar bears formidable predators, capable of killing a seal with a single blow from one of their huge paws or crushing its skull with their powerful jaws.

A polar bear may be seen swinging its head from side to side to hone in on a scent. Its sense of smell is so highly developed that it can smell carrion from up to 15 miles (24 kilometers) away. Its eyesight is especially good at detecting movement, and binocular vision enables it to judge distances well.

FIERCE ATTACKER

Compared with other bears, polar bears have more prominent canine teeth to cope with a meat diet. They also have well-developed incisors, which they use to remove the skin from the fat of seals as neatly as if they were using a pair of scissors.

Extremely sharp claws give the polar bear a firm grip, both on the ice and on its prey. The huge paws have thick hair between the pads, which provides insulation from the cold ice and also muffles the

This resourceful polar bear shows remarkable patience as it lies in wait by a seal's breathing hole. The bear lies on its belly on the ice, inching closer and closer to the hole as quietly as possible, until it is in prime position to pounce.

Illustration Douglas Ingram

SNIFFING THE AIR

Using its remarkably keen sense of smell, the bear locates a ringed seal pup in its birth lair, even beneath thick ice.

in SIGHT

Brett Froomer/Image Bank

IS IT A MYTH?

Many Arctic hunters believe that, when stalking seals, a polar bear will hide its prominent black nose behind one of its huge white forepaws in order to blend in with its surroundings. There is no direct evidence for this, but polar bears have been seen covering their muzzles with a paw on particularly cold days. This is to prevent heat being lost from their noses.

sound of its approach from its prey. Polar bear footpads have a natural nonslip surface. They are covered with thousands of minute soft projections, which create friction between the feet and the ice, and tiny pits that act like suction cups, increasing the grip. Its creamy-white fur helps camouflage the bear in its mainly white landscape.

Though generally seasonal, the food supply in the Arctic can be unpredictable, so the polar bear has adapted to take advantage of a glut of food. An adult can eat 10 percent of its body weight in just 30 minutes, and the stomach of a large male can hold as much as 220 pounds (90 kilograms) of food.

Although they are opportunist hunters—occasionally killing anything from voles, lemmings, ground squirrels, and birds to small whales—the staple diet of polar bears consists of seals, which make up over 90 percent of their food in most areas.

READY TO ATTACK

Rising up on its hind legs, the polar bear straightens itself up and raises its powerful forepaws high in the air. The bear needs all the weight of its huge body to succeed in the attack.

PREY

Though the polar bear's main prey are seals, it will hunt a wide variety of other animals and birds when food is scarce. In fact, polar bears will leap at the chance to catch anything that moves, from tiny lemmings to beluga whales.

Prey illustrations Ruth Grewcock

RINGED SEAL

BEARDED SEAL

Their favorite prey by far is the ringed seal, the most abundant marine mammal in the Arctic.

Ringed seals maintain breathing holes in the ice where they regularly surface for air. They keep the holes open by scraping with their flippers, which are equipped with large, strong nails. Adult seals prefer the stable ice off coastlines and in bays, while youngsters make do with areas of shifting, unstable ice. It is in these so-called "active zones" that bears do most of their hunting, since young and inexperienced seals are easier to catch.

Polar bears also prey on harp seals and hooded seals, sometimes killing large numbers of pups in breeding areas. In the western Arctic, especially in the Beaufort Sea off Northwest Canada, polar bears depend mainly on bearded seals for their food.

Polar bears are versatile and strategic hunters, able to outwit their prey in various ways. There are two basic methods—still-hunting and stalking. Still-hunting involves waiting next to a seal's breathing hole in the ice, or by the edge of open water, until the seal surfaces to breathe. Since the ice amplifies any sound, the bear must remain absolutely still, or the wary seal will be frightened off.

WAITING TO POUNCE

A polar bear's patience is remarkable: It will wait for hours near a breathing hole, lying on its belly with its chin on the ice. When a seal eventually surfaces, the bear springs into action, biting the victim on the head or body and throwing it out onto the ice. It finishes the seal off by biting it many more times on the head and neck. Still-hunting yields the highest return in food calories for the energy used.

THE CRUSHING BLOW

Dropping all of its weight through the thick ice roof of the birth lair, the bear is finally rewarded with its meal.

Illustrations Mike Donnelly/Wildlife Art Agency

HOODED SEAL	WALRUS CALF	BELUGA WHALE	EIDER DUCK	VOLE	LEMMING

Illustrations Mike Donnelly/Wildlife Art Agency

THE BIG FREEZE

Having spotted a beluga whale stranded in the shallows, the bear freezes. With its eyes fixed on its prey, it carefully plans its next move.

In spring, the polar bear focuses its attention on ringed seal pups, which are born in lairs dug out in the snow. The bear's acute sense of smell enables it to sniff out a seal pup in its lair from distances of 0.6 mile (1 kilometer) or more. Once it has honed in on its intended victim, it creeps up slowly and carefully, then stands stock-still. As soon as it hears the seal pup moving about, it stands up on its hind legs and

---

POLAR BEARS HUNT USING PATIENCE, STEALTH, AND CUNNING, CATCHING THEIR PREY DANGEROUSLY UNAWARES

---

crashes its forepaws down onto the roof of the lair. Often, the bear fails to break through the compacted snow at its first attempt, but it is usually rewarded with a kill sooner or later.

Stalking is more energetic than still-hunting and is used mainly in summer when the seals lie on the surface of the ice. As soon as it spots a seal, the bear freezes, sometimes in midstep, and decides how to approach. It then walks slowly toward its target, sometimes in a semicrouched posture. When it is about 50 to 100 feet (15 to 30 meters) away, the bear suddenly charges at top speed, seizing the seal with its teeth or claws before it can escape.

OUT OF SIGHT

A variation of stalking, though not a common one, involves an underwater approach. On spotting its prey, the polar bear slips noiselessly into the water and swims submerged between holes in the ice. When it surfaces to breathe, the bear lets only the tip of its nose break the water. As the bear reaches the seal, it claws its way onto the ice and leaps on its prey. However, the seal often gets away and, once it reaches the water, it can usually outswim the bear.

Sometimes in summer a bear will painstakingly

slide toward a seal along shallow channels and pools of meltwater that form on top of the sea ice, its body flattened like a great cream-colored rug.

Occasionally polar bears go for much bigger marine prey. In winter, groups of beluga whales may become trapped at a breathing hole when the surrounding sea freezes and they are unable to escape back to the ocean. At such times, polar bears strike the whales with their great forepaws and drag them out onto the ice. In summer, when belugas enter the mouths of Arctic rivers, some become stranded in the shallows and may fall prey to bears.

Polar bears relish carrion and will feed on any carcass they find. An Arctic fox or any other scavenger that ventures too close in its eagerness for scraps may be suddenly turned on and killed.

During summer in more southerly parts of their range, the ice melts and the polar bears can no longer get at seals. Then they must turn their attention to other prey. They hunt for voles and lemmings; they raid colonies of waterfowl, eating

Though the polar bear is partial to eating walrus pups, catching them is fraught with danger: the bear must first tackle the huge, powerful adults with their long, sharp tusks.

Nikita Ovsyanikov/Planet Earth Pictures

WHY BEARS ARE AGGRESSIVE

WITH ONE LEAP

the bear rushes toward its helpless victim, slashing its body with sharp claws. It drags the whale onto the ice before devouring it.

Bears can be among the most aggressive of all the carnivores—toward other bears, potential prey, and, on occasion, humans. The one reason, for both male and female bears, is connected with the drive to produce the maximum number of offspring. Bears are slow breeders and female bears are unable to give birth to more than a few cubs in a lifetime, typically as few as four to ten in the polar bear and six to eight in the grizzly. Therefore each cub is crucial to their overall reproductive success, and females will fiercely defend their young against any threat. Other bears, predators such as wolves, or humans who approach too close to a female with her cubs will be attacked and possibly wounded or killed.

Because mature female bears are scarce and hard to find, adult males mate with as many females as they can, only occasionally risking serious injury or death by fighting with equally strong rivals to defend a single female. Adult males also reduce competition by driving off or even killing subadult males that, if allowed to remain, would pose a threat when mature.

KEY FACTS

● A polar bear's sense of smell is so highly developed that it can sniff out a seal pup in its snow birth lair more than 6.5 ft (2 m) below the surface and can smell carrion from up to 15 miles (24 km) away.

● An adult polar bear needs an average of 11 lb (5 kg) of seal fat a day—equivalent to the amount of fat on one ringed seal pup—in order to survive. Eating an adult seal would give a bear enough energy to hunt for eleven days.

● Because Arctic prey is few and far between, polar bears take advantage of any kills they make and can eat up to 10 percent of their body weight in just thirty minutes.

● Up to 90 percent of the polar bear's diet is made up of seals. In milder regions, where there is less ice and therefore fewer seals, the bears must turn their attention to birds and small mammals.

incubating females and their eggs, and swim beneath ducks to pull them down under the water. Some polar bears in the Hudson Bay area of Canada specialize in hunting geese and ducks; birds form up to 70 percent of their diet.

CANNIBAL BEARS

Polar bears may also tackle large prey such as musk oxen on land, and cannibalism is not unknown; males will kill and eat cubs or even females. During the summer, polar bears will eat grass, berries, and other vegetation, including seaweed, which they consume with apparent relish.

After feeding, a polar bear removes all traces of greasy blubber, meat, and blood from its fur. In summer, it will wash in the water, but during the great winter freeze it makes do with rubbing its head in the snow and rolling around on its back. ■

LIFE CYCLE

Female polar bears breed only every three years, so competition between males is fierce. Often, two or more males come across the same female at the same time and bitter fighting may ensue. The bears grapple on the ice, lunging at each other with open jaws. The victor will stay with the female for a week or more, keeping other males away, while the pair mate many times over this period.

> THE ARCTIC CLIMATE IS SO HARSH THAT FEMALE POLAR BEARS MUST SHELTER WITH THEIR CUBS IN A DEN DUG OUT IN THE SNOW UNTIL SPRING ARRIVES

Although the bears mate in late April and May, the fertilized egg only begins to grow sometime in October. This process, known as delayed implantation, ensures that the development of the egg starts to take place only when the females have migrated back up north either to winter in last year's dens or to build new ones.

SAFE AND WARM

Pregnant females dig dens in snowdrifts around the end of October and remain inside until the cubs are born between late December and early January. About 75 percent of mothers give birth to twins, 20 percent to single cubs, and only 5 percent to triplets. The helpless newborn cubs are blind and deaf, with thin, white fur. To keep them warm, their mother cradles them into her body and, every so often, she lies on her back to allow them to suckle from one of the four nipples on her chest.

The mother suckles her young for up to two years and the cubs grow at a remarkable rate—polar bear milk is the richest of all terrestrial

AMAZING FACTS

SPECKS OF LIFE

All bear cubs are tiny at birth, but those of the polar bear are particularly minute. Little bigger than a rat and weighing about only 1 to 1.5 pounds (500 to 700 grams), they are the smallest newborn young relative to their mother's body size of any mammal besides marsupials. If newborn human babies were the same relative size, they would be only the size of your thumb!

YOUNGSTERS
closely follow their mother's tracks when they travel long distances across the ice and snow. They become independent at about two years old

RIDING HIGH
When traveling across deep snow or crossing a bay, a cub will often climb onto its mother's back and cling on with its sharp claws.

GROWING UP
The cubs stay close to their mother during their first few months. They will continue to suckle until they are two years old.

Illustrations Barry Croucher/Wildlife Art Agency

GROWING UP
The life of a young polar bear

NURSING CUBS

The mother suckles the tiny cubs at regular intervals. They will grow rapidly while being fed on her rich milk.

IN SPRING, *the female breaks out of the den and the three-month-old cubs begin to explore their new surroundings.*

Illustration Douglas Ingram

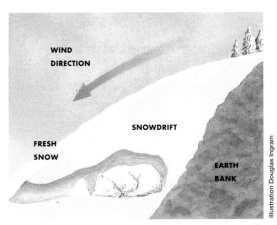

BREEDING DENS

Dens are dug in snowdrifts in the lee of hillocks, rocks, or cliffs where the wind will blow a layer of fresh snow over the top as a covering. The bear may plug the entrance of the den with a mound of snow to keep out the wind, and the warmth of its body will keep the interior snug. Dens may be as much as 40°F (20°C) or more warmer than the air outside.

Dens vary in shape and size, but their basic design is the same. An entry tunnel leads into a living chamber—typically about 5 to 7 feet (1.5 to 2 meters) across and 3 feet (1 meter) high—in which the cubs will be born, though females may enlarge their dens as winter progresses.

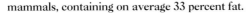

mammals, containing on average 33 percent fat.

At about a month old, the cubs can see and hear. By the time they are two months old, when they weigh some 12 to 15 pounds (5 to 7 kilograms), they start to explore the dark interior of the den, often digging out their own tunnels and small chambers.

Between late February and late April, the female breaks out of the den and the cubs emerge. Intensely curious about their surroundings, they frolic in the snow, chasing each other and sliding down slopes. However, the family often continues to shelter in the den for a week or two so that the cubs can become acclimatized to the bitter cold.

After having fasted for several months, the mother is ravenous, and as soon as possible she leads her offspring to the frozen sea and its abundance of seals. The nearest sea ice is usually

5 to 10 miles (8 to 16 kilometers) away, and the female regularly stops to allow her weary cubs a rest and a feed. Usually the cubs follow in their mother's tracks, but occasionally they ride on her back, clinging to her with their sharp claws.

When they reach the sea, the cubs watch the mother hunt and try to imitate her actions. Their early attempts at hunting are usually unsuccessful, because they are too impatient and the prey escapes.

ON THEIR OWN

At two years old, the cubs are able to hunt but they remain with their mother until she allows them to leave or until they are frightened off by a male who wants to mate with her.

Few polar bears live beyond 18 years of age in the wild, but some reach their twenties, and two have been found that were 32 years old. In zoos, polar bears have lived longer: One old male in London Zoo survived to the ripe old age of 41. ■

A FUTURE ON THIN ICE

PROTECTED FROM OVERHUNTING SINCE THE MID-1970S BY A UNIQUE INTERNATIONAL AGREEMENT, POLAR BEARS NOW FACE NEW THREATS FROM POLLUTION AND GLOBAL WARMING

About 4,000 years ago, distant ancestors of the present-day Inuits moved north from the great northern coniferous forests to begin a new way of life on the tundra and ice of the Arctic Ocean. They are thought to have spread from northeastern Siberia, crossing to North America via the ice of the Bering Sea. About a thousand years later, they developed harpoons in order to hunt the great bears, which, along with seals, caribou, and birds, became their means of survival in the harsh environment.

FIERCE COMPETITION

The huge white bears were formidable adversaries, especially to an unprotected human armed only with intelligence and a spear, and were competitors for the same staple food—seals. Legends indicate that the Inuit's ancestors learned a great deal about how to hunt seals from watching the bears.

The Inuits set out to hunt the bears on the ice in March and April. Typically, they would use a team

> THERE ARE MANY INUIT LEGENDS THAT REFER TO POLAR BEARS, SHORN OF THEIR HIDES, ASSUMING THE FORM OF HUMANS WHEN INSIDE THEIR OWN HOMES

of dogs to follow the bear's tracks. Then, when they were close enough, they would unleash the dogs, who would distract the bear by barking and biting at its heels. This would give the hunter a chance to move in close and kill the bear with a thrust from his lance or a shot from his bow.

The polar Inuit of Northwest Greenland hunted polar bears more than other indigenous peoples, who relied more on seals and caribou. But all these northern peoples held the bear in great esteem.

They believed the bears possessed souls, like the other animals they hunted, and they had many rituals to appease the powerful spirit of a slain bear to ensure future success in hunting.

ARCTIC INVASION

For centuries, subsistence hunting by native peoples using Stone Age weapons posed no great threat to the survival of the polar bear, but, from the 16th century on, with the advent of modern civilization and firearms, greater numbers of the bears began to be killed. European explorers ventured into the Arctic in search of the fabled Northwest Passage. Hunters and trappers invaded the region alongside them in search of arctic foxes, seals, and other fur-bearing animals.

Attracted by a ready food supply at explorer's camps and sealing stations, some bears were killed

The polar bear is of vital importance to the Inuit: It provides food, warm clothing, and fur rugs. Killing a bear is also considered a test of manhood.

Bryan and Cherry Alexander

The chart below shows the remarkable increase in the total world polar bear population, which has occurred since the mid-1960s.

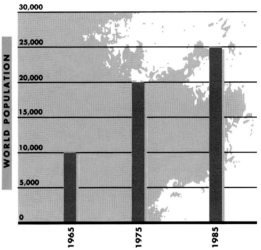

The Agreement on the Conservation of Polar Bears was signed by the five Arctic nations in 1973, though the Soviet Union had banned polar bear hunting as early as 1956. The agreement is widely viewed as a model of species and natural resource conservation.

● **It forbids the hunting of bears from aircraft and large motorized boats, allowing only limited subsistence hunting.**

● **It coordinates habitat protection, management, and research.**

The number of polar bear kills by country in the years leading up to the 1973 pan-Arctic agreement

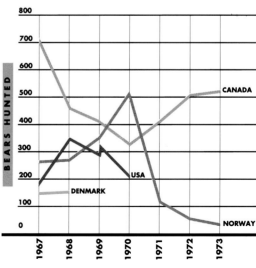

1687

ENDANGERED BY POLLUTION

in self-defense, but many more were shot to provide food for the men and their teams of sled dogs, as well as clothing. During the present century, trophy hunters began to venture into the Arctic, and with the aid of airplanes and snowmobiles they were able to reach prime polar bear habitat. Through the 1950s and 1960s, increasing numbers of bears were falling to their guns. In Alaska, the trophy kill rose from 139 in 1961 to 399 by 1966.

PUBLIC OUTCRY

Hunting with motorized equipment gave the bear little chance of escape. Two aircraft would take off together and fly out over the pack ice. When a bear was spotted, the plane containing the hunters landed while the other one drove the bear to within easy shooting distance. Even so, some of the more incompetent hunters were recorded as taking more than 20 shots to make their kill. As the value of polar

---

THERE SEEMED SOMETHING UNNATURAL TO MANY PEOPLE ABOUT THE OVERWHELMING TECHNOLOGY USED TO HUNT DOWN THIS GREAT PREDATOR

---

bear hides increased, the hunt organizers were able to charge up to $10,000 for a few days of "sport."

Tourists on board Norwegian ships near Svalbard, an island group north of Norway, were able to shoot polar bears on the pack ice, the bears having little chance of escape as they swam in the water. Trappers on Svalbard used "set-guns," unmanned traps where, attracted by bait, the bears triggered off a gun. This cruel method indiscriminately wounded or killed any bear that set the trap off, regardless of age or condition.

The public became outraged at the ways in which large numbers of polar bears were being legally killed. In response to this outcry, and the concerns of wildlife biologists throughout the Arctic, the first international meeting to discuss wildlife conservation was held in Fairbanks, Alaska, in 1965.

UNANIMOUS AGREEMENT

Attended by delegates from each of the Arctic nations with populations of polar bears—Norway, Denmark, the USSR, the United States, and Canada—it was agreed that each nation should take steps to conserve the species until the results of long-term research programs could be analyzed. The meeting also recommended that cubs and females with cubs should be protected throughout the year.

Further meetings paved the way for the International Agreement on the Conservation of Polar Bears and their Habitat, which was signed on

NASA/Science Photo Library

THE DISAPPEARING WORLD OF THE POLAR BEAR

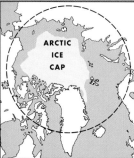

Many climatologists predict that the polar regions—and the animals that live there—will be the first to feel the effects of global warming. Even an increase in average temperature of just a few degrees could alter the distribution of sea ice, proving disastrous for the highly specialized animals that live there, which require a stable climate in order to breed successfully. Because polar bears are almost completely dependent on a single food source—the ringed seal—they are particularly vulnerable to such effects.

GLOBAL WARMING

When the earth's surface is warmed by the sun's rays, most of the energy is absorbed and the rest is radiated back into space. The combination of gases makes sure that most of the heat stays within the earth's atmosphere, helping to maintain a stable average temperature.

This "greenhouse effect" is vital to life on earth, but some human activities are accelerating the process. Huge amounts

A GOLDEN FUTURE? A POLAR BEAR MOTHER WITH HER CUBS MAKES HER WAY ACROSS THE SUN-DRENCHED ICE CAP.

CONSERVATION MEASURES

● Greenpeace, Friends of the Earth, and other environmental groups have long campaigned for changes in government policies aimed at reducing levels of carbon dioxide emissions and developing sustainable energy policies.

● Countries such as Denmark and Holland and the state of California lead the world in renewable energy policies involving wind

of the greenhouse gases—carbon dioxide, chlorofluorocarbons (CFCs), methane, nitrous oxide, and low-level ozone—are being pumped into the atmosphere, and this may result in a rise in the earth's average temperature.

At present the polar ice reflects most of the sun's heat back into space, but as the planet slowly warms up and the ice caps start melting, the dark rocks beneath will absorb the sun's heat. This may in turn warm the earth still further, so that more ice will melt, more rock will be exposed, more heat will be retained, and so on in an endless spiral that threatens disaster.

Carbon dioxide—which is produced by burning fossil fuels is, it is suggested, responsible for up to half the increase in global warming. A quarter was due to CFCs used in aerosols, refrigerators, and air conditioners, but the use of CFCs is now strongly discouraged.

François Gohier/Auscape International

and solar energy. They produce as much as 10 percent of total energy levels from renewable sources. At the moment, few other countries have the resources or the will to develop such projects.

● Denmark aims to reduce its carbon dioxide emissions by at least 20 percent by the year 2005 in the first stage of a move away from fossil fuel dependency.

POLAR BEARS IN DANGER

THE INTERNATIONAL UNION FOR THE CONSERVATION OF NATURE (IUCN) CLASSIFIES THE STATUS OF POLAR BEARS AS VULNERABLE. THIS MEANS THAT THE ANIMAL IS LIKELY TO MOVE INTO THE ENDANGERED CATEGORY IF PRESENT CONDITIONS CONTINUE AS THEY ARE. IF IT WERE TO FALL INTO THE ENDANGERED CATEGORY, THE BEARS' SURVIVAL WOULD BE UNLIKELY UNLESS STEPS WERE TAKEN TO SAVE IT.

POLAR BEAR	VULNERABLE

THIS MAY SEEM SOMEWHAT CONFUSING, SINCE HUNTING LIMITATIONS WERE IMPOSED AND POLAR BEAR POPULATIONS HAVE ACTUALLY INCREASED. EVEN SO, THEIR FUTURE IS BOUND UP WITH THE ARCTIC ITSELF, WHICH WILL BECOME INCREASINGLY VULNERABLE TO POLLUTION AND MINERAL EXPLOITATION.

Stephen Krasemann/NHPA

November 15, 1973, in Oslo, Norway. In 1976, it was ratified by the governments of the five Arctic nations and came into effect. In 1981, at the end of the agreed five-year trial period, the agreement was unanimously reaffirmed for an indefinite period.

This remarkable example of international cooperation is unique in that it represents the first time the five Arctic nations have agreed on any subject affecting the region. Moreover, its approach toward conservation was both practical and scientific, two factors that helped to guarantee its remarkable success.

Although the agreement does permit a limited amount of hunting, it sets out strict conditions under which this may take place. The bears may be taken only by local hunters exercising traditional rights and using traditional methods, or for genuine scientific research, to prevent serious disturbance to the management of other resources, or for the protection of life and property.

CONTINUING TRADITION

Today, though rifles have replaced the spear and the bow and arrow, and though snowmobiles are often used instead of dog teams, the subsistence hunting of polar bears remains an important activity among the Inuits of Greenland, Canada, and Alaska. The agreement has allowed Inuit hunters to become directly involved with the management of polar bears and other Arctic wildlife, with positive results for conservation.

Another part of the agreement concerns the protection of the Arctic ecosystems on which the bears depend. Important habitats have been set aside for conservation in Greenland, Canada,

ALONGSIDE MAN

PROBLEM BEARS

The small town of Churchill, Manitoba, on the western shore of Canada's Hudson Bay, is known as the polar bear capital of the world. In autumn, bears visit the town's landfill, feeding on anything from scraps of meat to pieces of plastic.

A "jail" has now come into operation in the town, capable of holding 16 adult bears, including 4 mothers and their cubs. When bears enter Churchill, they are captured and held in the jail until the sea freezes over again and they can be released out on the ice. The bears are not fed while they are in jail, however, as feeding would provide a reward that might attract them back.

Joel Bennett/Survival Anglia

Conrad Wothe/Survival Anglia

Svalbard, and Wrangel and Gerald Islands in Russia's eastern Siberia.

Conducting accurate censuses of polar bears in the vast, inhospitable Arctic habitat is extremely difficult. Today, the total population of polar bears is estimated at between 20,000 and 40,000. But even if the numbers were known accurately, this is not necessarily a great help in conserving the species. It is just as important to learn about trends within the separate subpopulations.

PATIENT STUDY

Biologists who study polar bears need a great deal of patience, as Arctic storms can delay access to a study area for a couple of weeks or more. Research is expensive, since aircraft are usually needed to reach the bears. It also brings its own dangers: In

A mother and her cubs scavenge food from one of Churchill's dumps, but their freedom is short-lived as they are towed away to "jail."

A researcher tattoos a bear's inner lip. Layers around the canine tooth reveal the bear's age.

October 1990, two Alaskan bear researchers and their pilot disappeared, never to return.

Over the last twenty-five years or so, safe, reliable tranquilizing drugs have been developed and methods of darting the animal refined so that individuals can be studied and followed. Satellite tracking of the bears has also revolutionized the process. Radio collars, which weigh only 4 pounds

> THE TECHNOLOGY THAT ONCE THREATENED THE VERY EXISTENCE OF THE POLAR BEAR IS NOW BEING USED TO ENSURE ITS SURVIVAL

(1.8 kilograms) and last up to 18 months, send signals to a satellite orbiting the poles that transmits the animal's location to a receiving station. This new technology can even give an idea of how accurate—within 500 to 3,300 feet (150 to 1,000 meters)—the location is, as well as details of the bear's temperature and its activity level. All this information is then relayed to the researchers in the form of computer plots of the bear's movements.

Consequently, more is now known about the polar bear than ever before. Its many admirers are hoping such information will be put to good use. ∎

Dan Guravich/ Photo Researchers/Oxford Scientific Films

INTO THE FUTURE

Although current polar bear populations seem fairly healthy, and hunting is at a very low level and well controlled, a number of threats loom on the horizon: The bears are vulnerable to habitat loss, pollution, and a diminishing food source because of the mass death of seals from viruses caused by pollution.

Industrial pollutants such as PCBs (waste products of the plastic industry) and the pesticide DDT are increasingly released into the world's oceans, including the Arctic. They are believed to affect an animal's ability to reproduce, which could be particularly devastating for polar bears since they are by nature slow breeders, and thus could lead to a rapid population decline.

This is not the only effect of PCBs. Research suggests that they also impair the development of young, damage the immune system, cause cancers,

PREDICTION

CLOSER TO HOME

In the aftermath of the Gulf War, Canadian and United States oil companies will be more eager than ever to exploit the resources of their Arctic territories, thereby ensuring a domestic oil supply unaffected by the unstable politics of the Middle East.

damage the nervous system, and affect the liver, kidneys, and other organs.

These pollutants build up in the food chain and are at their most toxic in the diet of the habitat's top predators. Bears in Svalbard are particularly affected, and the Norwegian Polar Institute is deeply concerned about their future ability to reproduce.

The increasing popularity of tourism geared to enabling people to encounter wild polar bears in their natural habitat also raises potential problems, especially among vital summering habitats. However, these northern safaris also have their benefits. They can bring in much-needed income to such places as Churchill in Canada as motels, restaurants, and stores are filled with people hoping to see Arctic animals in their natural environment.

If such developments are run with the bear's welfare at heart, they can only serve to increase the popularity of this already much-loved animal and increase general concern for its conservation. ■

Illustration Brin Edwards/Wildlife Art Agency

SOVIET BREAKUP

Recently, concern has been expressed about the impact of the breakup of the former Soviet Union on Russia's polar bears. With 4,000 miles (6,500 kilometers) of Arctic coastline, Russia may hold as many as 10,000 bears. The increasing economic chaos that has resulted from the breakdown in central authority has led to illegal hunts and bear poaching. High levels of chemical and radioactive pollution have also been revealed to exist in the Russian Arctic.

Despite these problems, the breakup has brought a new openness to scientific cooperation. Increased opportunities for western bear biologists to meet with their Russian counterparts means an expansion in research and management of bear populations. And a bear park has been proposed for the Bering Strait region between Russia and Alaska, to provide much-needed protection for the area's bears.

OIL PRODUCTION

In the Beaufort Sea region of Canada, polar bear migration routes overlap with an area that has great potential for offshore oil drilling. Not far to the west, the Arctic National Wildlife Refuge in Alaska, a major denning area, is the most promising site for oil and gas prospecting in the United States.

An uncontrolled oil blowout under the ice during winter or spills from vessels carrying oil from such sites might not only threaten the polar bears themselves but could also dramatically reduce the seal populations on which the bears are almost wholly dependent.

Bryan and Cherry Alexander

INDEX

Published by Marshall Cavendish Corporation
99 White Plains Road
Tarrytown, New York 10591-9001

© Marshall Cavendish Corporation, 1997
© Marshall Cavendish Ltd, 1994

The material in this series was first published in the English language by Marshall Cavendish Limited, of 119 Wardour Street, London W1V 3TD, England.

Library of Congress Cataloging-in-Publication Data

Encyclopedia of mammals.
p. cm.
Includes index.
ISBN 0-7614-0575-5 (set)   ISBN 0-7614-0586-0 (v. 11)

Summary: Detailed articles cover the history, anatomy, feeding habits, social structure, reproduction, territory, and current status of ninety-five mammals around the world.
1. Mammals—Encyclopedias, Juvenile. [1. Mammals—Encyclopedias.] I. Marshall Cavendish Corporation.
QL706.2.E54 1996
599'.003—dc20
                                                                    96-17736
                                                                      CIP
                                                                      AC

Printed in Malaysia
Bound in U.S.A.